D1630087

2.2.

SOCCER FROM
THE PRESS BOX

Three of the great figures in modern football:
on the right is Willie Steffen of Switzerland, on
the left is Tommy Lawton of England, and the
man in the centre with both feet off the ground
is Parola of Italy. The incident is from the
Great Britain v. Rest of Europe match at
Hampden Park, Glasgow, May 1947.

Photo: Daily Record, Glasgow.

SOCCER

FROM
THE

PRESS
BOX

by

ARCHIE LEDBROOKE
and
EDGAR TURNER

Nicholas Kaye
London

First published by Nicholas Kaye Ltd.,
Trebeck Street, London, W.1.

1950

Copyright 1950 by Nicholas Kaye Ltd.

This book may not be reproduced by any means in whole or
in part without permission. Application with regard to
copyright should be addressed to the publishers.

740

Printed for Nicholas Kaye Ltd.
at the Yorkdale Press, Thornton Road, Bradford.

CONTENTS

LIST OF ILLUSTRATIONS

INTRODUCTION

THERE are two ways of writing about a football match. You can watch the game as ninety minutes of sport, and treat it as a piece of entertainment complete in itself. Or you can attempt to relate the match to all the football preceding it in seventy or eighty years of organised Association Football. It is the view of the writers that every match, every transfer and every bit of legislation, have a place in the larger framework, and the notes which make up this book are the result of thinking aloud over a number of years of watching football from press boxes in various parts of the world.

As the penny popular newspaper dealt with more and more with sport, realising that a new public had grown up, it was inevitable that the number of sporting journalists should increase and that their scope should be widened. Nowadays every representative football team to go abroad takes with it a quota of reporters and at home an event such as the Cup Final is attended by upwards of two hundred men from newspapers of varying degrees of importance and style and whose treatment of the game will vary according to the method of the writers and the class of publication they represent.

As sporting journalism grew, so naturally it changed. One has the impression that fifty years ago the men who covered football knew legislators better than they knew the players with the exception of a chosen few, a handful of internationals with whom the journalists seemed on terms of intimacy. Then came a stage when descriptions of the play were of paramount importance, because newspapers (referring now to the nationals, and not to the specialist sporting journals) were bigger, gave a deal of space, and there was room for descriptive writing. Then came a spell when the transfer fee story seemed to over-ride all other interests, only for a new trend to follow it during the semi-exhibition games of the Second World War. It became the fashion for the reporter to enter the dressing-room to talk to players, to ask their opinions, and to quote them, a development which surely represents a step backwards in the development of the art of reporting?

A pupil of the late J. A. H. Catton once said that he was told by that strange little man to say in his report: **What** happened, **how** it happened ,and **why** it happened," and that pithy instruction would seem to hold good for other events on the newspaper diary than merely sporting fixtures. An experienced and skilled football reporter is presumably paid by his newspaper to tell of what he sees, and if his energies are primarily directed thus, he would seem to be going a long way towards earning his money.

Another sequel to the granting of further space to sport by the national newspapers was the greater interest taken in reporting by the players themselves. Doubtless they always took heed of what was written, but in recent years many professionals have shown a touchy reaction to the printed word. They devour all that is written about them, they keep their own books of cuttings, and if they don't . . . well, there is always some kind " friend " who produces his wallet and asks if the unfortunate player has seen this or that particular cutting. . . .

Not unnaturally a player may sometimes show resentment when criticism is printed, whether it be from a comparitively unskilled reporter or from an experienced writer whose opinion, backed by many years of observation and perhaps a flair for the game, may be all the more hurtful. On the whole players hide their resentment pretty well. Disputes between players and journalists are happily rare, and most of the players, being gentlemen too, grant the journalists the doubt of being honest.

To some footballers, criticism is the splendid spur. Mr. Tom Whittaker, speaking to football writers not so long ago, stated without qualification that at the beginning of the season 1949-50, his own Arsenal players found it so. In the early weeks of the season Arsenal were an indifferent team, it will be recalled. Mr. Whittaker declared that some of his players, reading the criticism voiced of their individual play, re-acted quickly. They accepted the criticism and determined that they would show that they could do better, that their current form was not their true form.

Developing his theme, the distinguished manager, whose team were to win the F.A. Cup the following day, paid a tribute to what the Press had done for soccer, and he added that the part played by newspapers was possibly more appreciated in other countries. He recalled that when he took Arsenal to Brazil, he was checking up the accounts for one match when he came across an item allowing expenses for 20 journalists to travel by air to report the game. It was apparently accepted that this was a proper charge against the gate.

Tom Whittaker was good enough to add, too, that when his telephone rang at home (and goodness knows how frequently that may be, or at what unreasonable hours) he always tried to supply the news.

The actual reporting of a football match—that is, describing the play as distinct from writing about team selections, transfers, international aspects, and so on—should be easy to a trained journalist. Broadly speaking there are four kinds of report covering a normal Saturday afternoon League match.

(a) The evening paper report, on sale soon after the game thas ended.

(b) The Sunday paper story, in many cases rushed over within minutes of the final whistle, at best written within an hour and a half of the end.

(c) The Monday morning story, written when the reporter has had time to think over the game between its end and his arrival at the office on Sunday afternoon.

(d) The running commentary put out over the radio.

Opinions may differ on the difficulty of producing these reports, and of their value. The opinion is here given that the running commentary put out by the radio is the easiest and least valuable, and that the Sunday paper report is perhaps the most difficult. Let us give some reasons for that opinion.

The radio reporter, sitting in front of a microphone or with a hand instrument clapped close to his mouth, has only one job. He has to tell of what he is seeing from kick to kick, and if a reporter cannot do that, then he is not a good reporter. The evening newspaper man usually has a telephone in front of him so that he can dictate his report without writing it out in full, and in that he chiefly tells the story of the play, his work is similar to that of the radio commentator. But whereas the latter gushes along at anything from 150 to 300 words a minute, without any limitations of space due to the size of the newspaper column, the evening paper reporter has to be selective. With perhaps a limit of 2,000 words on his report, he must choose only the significant incidents, or the amusing ones, and as he has at best only minutes in which to choose, and frequently seconds, he must be a shrewd observor and a trained reporter if he is to do his work well.

14

Moreover, since the printed word must of necessity create and leave a stronger impression than the spoken word, he must be more careful in his choice of phrases, paying attention to the finer shades of meaning. And since frequently his newspaper circulates in an area of partisan interest he will be expected to intersperse with his descriptive stuff a few lines here and there of general criticism and appreciation.

The evening newspaper report, although completed in such similar circumstances so similar to those surrounding the radio running commentary, is therefore normally far more valuable. In fact, the running commentary, first-class entertainment though it may be, is in many cases completely valueless to the student of football.

Five minutes after the last whistle the radio reporter will be getting his breath back and the evening paperman tucking his telephone into its little case under the seats in the press box. About the same time the Sunday newspaperman is tearing up his first attempt and starting again unless he is having one of those lucky days when the thing goes sweetly from the first sentence.

In the good Sunday paper report the writer will be expected to fulfill the Catton method of What-How-Why, and he will have precious little time in which to sort out the How and Why. His report will be phoned to his office as speedily as possible because Sunday newspapers run many different editions, have a complicated circulation problem, and are therefore produced and printed at break-neck speed.

The Sunday newspaper sports editor wants something else, however. He will usually call for the report to be colourful—not coloured in the sense of being one-sided, but written in a style which will make for easy reading and which will match up to the style of writing employed on the other pages of the same newspaper.

The man writing for Monday morning has up to 24 hours to think about the match if necessary, and so far that is a help rather than a hindrance. But he has this difficulty: the radio, the evenings, and the Sundays—all have had their say. He must be careful, while telling the truth and dealing with basically the same facts, that he does not merely repeat what they have said. He must not be the gramophone on which the same record is played.

In the search for a new " angle " for Monday morning there lies a danger that the reporter may dwell overmuch on trifles to the exclusion of essentials. There is the danger that he may be compelled to elevate a matter of little significance to headline status. To keep his story sane, but different, is a difficult job.

In fact, the reporter's job is as difficult as the player's, and for this reason: a footballer, playing before a crowd, is working in public. A clerk, an engineer, an accountant, a draughtsman, does not work in the full view of the public. A player does, and a reporter too, to the extent that his finished work is **immediately** put on show. There is little time for revision, precious little for those second thoughts which are proverbially the best.

If therefore, the football fan who reads a report of a match—one of those reports written against the clock—disagrees with the verdict or believes that a single incident has been wrongly described or interpreted, he should, before embarking on a too-severe criticism, ask himself this question: " Could I, at my particular job, put up an equally good show if I were compelled to work against time, all the time? "

The reporter, like the games player (and the stage player, too) tries to keep the show going against all difficulties.

We like to believe, and are proud to say, that the journalists we know and meet in press boxes are good troupers.

PART ONE

Great Argument

by

EDGAR TURNER

THE CASE OF NEIL FRANKLIN

A blow for the freedom
of the British footballer.

WHEN Neil Franklin and George Mountford closed
their homes and flew off with their families to Colombia, they symbolised the fight which the Players'
Union have consistently made for the freedom of the
footballer. After two months Franklin's dream was
ended. He flew back with his wife and was suspended
for his Bogota adventure. Roy Paul and Jack Headley
went to Colombia and back without signing up and
Billy Higgins also returned. Mountford, Charlie
Mitten and Bobby Flavell, however, stayed on.
The outstanding thing was the significance of it
all—that could not be lost on anyone.

Soccer received the biggest jolt for many a year,
and the Players Union became armed with the most
powerful weapon they had yet had. It was a complete
parallel to the occasion when American baseball
players slipped into Mexico until salaries had been
revised back home. Now, the pay of those American
baseball players is held up as the perfect example by
British footballers.

Franklin has already described the terms under
which he went to the Santa Fe club—£3,000 paid into
his account, £300 a month, £56 bonuses for helping
to win his first two matches, £150 or more bonus for
winning a needle match, in addition to other per-
quisites and cut-price luxury cars. It was enough to
make any footballer's mouth water.

B

England badly missed Franklin in Portugal and Belgium. His departure could not have come at a more dramatic moment with the World Cup Finals at Rio to follow, though Sante Fe did signify their willingness to release him for that fiesta. But despite all the inducement which is offered, the opportunity for a general clear-out of British players to Colombia does not exist. It is only a small footballing country.

Moreover, although they might skim a little cream off British football, there will always be young talent to take the place of anyone who may go off to Bogota or elsewhere.

It is interesting to recall that before Neil packed up and flew off, Jock Dodds had done it in a smaller degree two or three years previously, when he refused to re-sign for Blackpool and went to play for the Eire club, Shamrock Rovers. It was during that time that Britain returned to F.I.F.A., which now virtually controls the game throughout the World. Thus the door was closed, Dodds returned, and British and Eire clubs sighed with relief, although many English clubs had not been averse to getting Irish players for nothing. Colombia is the latest chink in the F.I.F.A. armour, and through it, Franklin and the others went. Now, more strenuous efforts than ever are being made to get the whole of the football world organised within F.I.F.A. but that will not stop British players from seeking a revision of contracts which will enable them to make their own terms

Franklin received not only a fabulous down-payment with glittering " perks " but a contract which was renewable every twelve months. And there are only 28 League matches in Colombian football against 42 in England. A footballer is no different from the vast majority of people. He finds it irksome to be tied body and soul to one club. He wishes to be free.

That is why the Players' Union presses for the private contract, whereby a player can make his own terms with a club as to payment and duration of services—in other words, no fixed maximum (like the present £12 a week), and freedom to sign for six months, twelve months, five years, or ten, according to his own fancy (and a club's willingness).

In order to get his present position quite clear, it is necessary to recapitulate several things. First of importance is that under Football League law, a player may receive only a £10 signing-on fee, whether he is a raw recruit or a man who is transferred from one club to another for a record sum.

That £10 is a paltry figure for the big clubs, but it is still a form of protection for the smaller ones who cannot afford big signing-on fees. But what a comparison to Franklin's £3,000 signing-on fee!

Franklin's exodus from British football occurred on Sunday, May 7. The Football League held their annual meeting on June 3—twenty-seven days after his departure, and at a time when every newspaper in the country was carrying stories of his experiences in Bogota and when it was known that Stoke City had, presumably to safeguard transfer rights, sent him an offer to re-sign for them. Yet at the League annual meeting no one considered it necessary to bring up an emergency resolution to provoke discussion.

Football is notoriously slow to move, and the rulers of the game may argue that it has developed so wonderfully as public entertainment, their refusal to dash into new legislation from time to time has proved the correct course.

When Franklin's case was not mentioned at the annual meeting it was suggested one of two things: either the League believed that the number of footballers who go abroad were so few that there was no problem (!) or else they were determined that the players themselves should fire the next shots.

Noteworthy, too, at the meeting was the refusal of the clubs to accept a proposal for an amnesty on illegal payments, to be followed by stern action for the next offender caught out.

Under pressure from the Players' Union, the present League contract has been altered from one which ended when the season finished in May to one which terminates at the end of July. That was because it was contended that the new form would provide a salary for twelve months of the year and a safeguard against clubs who did not re-sign their players immediately the season finished.

Apart from the League contract, on which he is technically retained, there is another—a Football Association form, on which he is technically signed and re-signed, as the case may be. Now, that F.A. form is just as important as the League one, because if it is overlooked by a club, a player who so wishes could escape into non-League football.

By a certain date each year, a club must notify the F.A. of the players it wishes to re-sign. If they fail to do that, then a player is given a loophole to go into non-League football.

Then there is the case of the player who is " for transfer " and the one on the transfer list. There is a subtle difference. If he is 'for transfer' he is still firmly retained by his club, but if he is placed on the transfer list it means that a club may not pay him wages after his contract expires and if he is not transferred to, or signed by, another League club, he is free to go into non-League football.

One of the contentions of the Players' Union is that clubs ought to continue paying a man his wages if they place him on the transfer list until he gets another job, but that has drawbacks into which it is not proposed to go in this discussion.

Post-war Soccer, like all other popular forms of sport, is enjoying a terrific boom. Those million-odd gates a week which are bringing in big profits, resulting in tremendous transfer fees, are having an unsettling effect on the player, who feels that as he is the one who is attracting the public, he ought to have a bigger " cut " of what is coming in.

In a situation whereby too much money chases too few goods, there is always the danger of a vicious spiral and under-the-counter methods, and few people in the game deny that Soccer is immune from such an experience. Talk has been quite open of players who have " touched " clubs eager to sign them for anything from a few pounds to a few thousands (by some method or other).

The stories of the player's second-hand motor-car worth no more than £200 being sold for over £1,000, and the player whose mongrel dog was offered for £500 are now well-known. Unfortunately, these things are difficult to prove, but the football authorities are not asleep. Proof of just one good case might blow the lid off the game. Already, there is talk of clubs who will not make irregular payments banding themselves into an association to fight those who may be tempted to do so.

Illegal payments and illegal approaches to players are not new—they have been one of the problems of the game for long enough—but there never has been such fierce discussion about it all. To quote the old proverb: " Where there's smoke there's fire. . . . "

Suspension from the game for life could be the absolute penalty. Certain it is that the game must be kept clean, but even so, it is still one of the straightest in world sport to-day.

Under the private contract, whereby a player would be free to negotiate his own terms, the question of irregular payments as now discussed would not arise.

It is argued by many players—but not all—that they are public entertainers like boxers and stage stars, but there is, in fact, quite a difference. A boxer generally has a shorter life than a footballer and far less security. Between his fights he has to keep himself, his manager, a large **entourage** and pay all his own training expenses. All that is quite a "headache" which the footballer never has to face.

So far as the stage artist is concerned, he usually reaches his peak at a much later age than the footballer, who, like John Charles, of Leeds United, for example, can be a star at 17 years of age. Furthermore, the stage artist is a public performer six nights of the week with two matinees thrown in. On the whole, his life is much harder than the Soccer player's, what with theatrical "digs" and constant travelling month in, month out.

The most important thing, however, is that the footballer must essentially be a team man. He may be an attractive performer, but he cannot play without ten colleagues, and it is upon that team spirit, which money cannot buy, that the success of a side lies. Would it be politic, therefore, to pay one footballer more than another?

"No," say some people.

"Yes," say others, and quote the very good case of Scottish football, where some men **are** paid more than others without ill-effects.

The case of the Scottish footballer—many of whom, however, are not loath to move into English Soccer with its equal-pay-for-all—rather strikes at the opinion that if a footballer got the private contract he would constantly be on the move from one club to another, chasing the money. But it is a danger.

So the main problem is: How can a star footballer, who **does** help to draw crowds, be paid a sum worthy of his services and yet retain his loyalty to one club?

Many people have offered many suggestions, one of which has been that players might share in a percentage of profits at the end of each season. Idea is to give a minimum wage, so that whatever happens, the player would be assured of a livelihood. Then it would be up to the players themselves to put money into their own pockets by playing attractive football and attracting the best possible crowds.

It is even suggested that the minimum scale should alter according to the division—First, Second, or Third—in which a team plays. That is, say, a £10 minimum for the First Division, £8 for the Second Division, and £6 for the Third Division, with scales worked out commensurately for the reserve players, or first team appearances.

Therefore, players would be rewarded for getting into the higher division, and penalised for dropping into the lower ones. The same thing would apply in relation to the additional profits-sharing scheme.

But even in that there are snags. It is believed that the desire for points to get into a higher division or save a club from relegation would be even greater than now, and would lead to rougher play; furthermore, that players would want to move to the clubs showing the biggest profits.

That is just one of many suggestions. Here are three more, the first from a player, the second from a manager, and the third from a director:—

Stanley Mortensen (Blackpool and England).

" With the game booming, many clubs are showing big profits which holds out hope of higher pay for professionals. I have always urged with such powers as I possess that every man in a professional team should receive the same pay for playing in the same match. I think it makes for team-work. There may be stars, but the eleventh man works as hard as the rest in actual playing conditions.

"My idea, therefore, is this: that players who wish should attend the F.A. coaching courses and then, on being passed out with some kind of qualification, be placed on a League list of 'qualified men,' then, when a number of first-team games have been completed, say 150, to guarantee efficiency and experience, merit money should become payable either by the clubs or the League from a central fund.

"If 400 players were in receipt of £1 a week extra at one time, this would surely not prove an intolerable burden to the Football League.

"Something like £100,000 must go through the turnstiles each week, so a cut of one half of one per cent, would do the trick. Moreover, the scheme would surely tend to raise the standard of play and the status of professional players, and as such is the only scheme I know which would give more money to the players and help to improve soccer.

"This scheme also meets the complaint so frequently made against present conditions of professional football: that after a man has reached the age of 24 or so, he never gets a rise in wages. The maximum is a maximum, and there it is.

"There are few other walks of life in which this same frustration applies.

"The scheme could be added to. After another 100 games the equivalent of three seasons, allowing for injuries—a player might be allowed to go on a refresher course to adapt himself to changed conditions and new methods of coaching, and become entitled, on passing, to a further increment on his pay. So the player staying in the game would have rises of pay commensurate with his experience and proved ability to receive ideas.

" I firmly believe this is one way in which the Football Association and the Football League could co-operate to the betterment of the welfare of players and the raising of standard of soccer. Every player would be anxious to qualify as soon as possible, and would naturally feel proud of his status when passed out as a merit man."

Mr. Cliff Britton (Everton Manager).

" One of the finest things in player-club relationships is loyalty and I think there should be greater rewards for the loyal footballer. Under present regulations, a player who has given first-class service may receive £750 every five years. Not many players receive two benefits, and it's practically a miracle if a man gets three.

" Now, if a player has given such service that he qualifies for a second benefit, I think he ought to receive double the amount of his first—that is, £1,500 —but only if he qualifies for it with one club. By doing that, he has proved his loyalty, and, therefore should be well rewarded. I feel that it would make men more settled."

Mr. Hilton Crowther (Leeds United Director).

" I am in favour of a system in which a player gets a rise in wages every time he re-signs for his club. If he is transferred on the initiative of his club, his wages are maintained at the level he has reached, and continued with his new club from that stage; if he is transferred at his own request, his wages go back to basic pay."

ALL those are very good points—for those clubs who can afford it. In legislating for the player on this vexatious question, the authorities, however, have to bear in mind that neither one club, nor a dozen, make the game. There are 92 League clubs. Would all those others be able to fall into line with such schemes? Already, there are one or two feeling the pinch in having to pay four per cent of their " gates " to the players' provident scheme.

Furthermore, there is another important aspect. In this fair-shares-for-all world, the football spectator who for so long has endured his football snivelling in the rain on roofless terraces, will demand more and more comfort—covered accommodation especially. The clubs are aware of it, and as soon as building restrictions are lifted, have plans for improving their grounds. All that will take money—big money.

The League President has already stated that this is a " phoney period " in the transfer situation. The players may get more money—like everyone else, they are entitled to everything they can secure—but whatever is done must be something which will be durable. Hasty decisions now might ruin the whole game. It is to be hoped that a satisfactory solution will be found to the biggest problem in the game.

THIS THING CALLED SLAVERY

The facts of wages, bonuses, and benefits.

HOWEVER footballers may be hamstrung by present agreements and however desirable it may be, all things considered, to revise those agreements, players are not quite the downtrodden individuals many people are led to believe. Football clubs neither here, in Colombia, or elsewhere are philanthropic institutions, and they themselves would be the first to admit it. Soccer has grown into a tremendous spectacle and clubs must conduct their affairs like the best business houses. They must have a shop window and into that window must go the best goods—in this instance, the players, of course—to attract more and more customers.

It is said that there is no sentiment in business, but many a club has suffered by allowing sentiment too free a hand. Like different business firms, some clubs treat their players better than those with other clubs, but there is not one which purposely sets out to victimise its staff and create a bad impression. Such a thing would be nothing short of disastrous to happy player-club relationships, without which there could be no loyalty and keen enterprise.

There are, of course, some clubs who stick rigidly to law and order, against which the usual easy-going nature of the sportsman (and others who dislike discipline) rebels. Whatever policy is pursued is up to the club itself. Each one is a separate cell or community which helps to build up the whole pattern of the game.

All this, the player, his parents, guardians, or friends, should know before a man ever signs a con-

SOCCER FROM THE PRESS BOX

tract to join a club. The footballer to-day prides himself upon being better educated and more enlightened than his predecessor, so that there is less excuse for him than at any time in the history of the game.

Maybe some footballers have been badly done by in the past, but never at any time has he been compelled to stay in the game, or even enter the game, if he did not wish to. It is important to get this clearly in mind: a man enters football of his own volition and can leave it any time he likes.

No one can **make** him play if he doesn't want to. He does so either for his enjoyment, to suit his own interests in some way or other, because he feels he can earn a better living at it than at other things, or as a means to supplement an income already derived from a different source or sources.

All that can apply to a few so-called amateurs, too, as the F.A. occasionally proves. But let's stick to the professionals, who on the whole get a better deal and a far easier time from their employers than most types of workers. For instance, how would you like a job with these conditions:—

(a) £1,200 a year income;

(b) Work for two hours a day;

(c) Be entertained practically every other week-end at your firm's expense;

(d) Spend a fortnight nearly every year on a tour abroad (again at the firm's or someone else's expense);

(e) Have three months' summer holiday;

(f) Rent a fully-furnished £1,500 house (and better) at 25s. a week;

(g) Receive various free meals and entertainment; and

(h) Be presented every Christmas with a turkey?

All those things, a top-class player with a little luck can get **from soccer alone.** All that is permissibe, within the rules—nothing off-the-side, or under-the-counter about it. Here is a full explanation underneath each sub-heading:—

£1,200 a year income.

In all fairness, it should be stated that a man must not only be a top-class player himself, but must belong to a club capable of winning all the honours for an income like this to be earned. It includes his salary, his bonuses, his benefits, and everything that it is possible to earn, including the new 10 per cent tax free provident scheme. It can be made up like this:—

Salary at £12 a week during the playing season and £10 a week during the close season	£	590
Every five years a club may pay a £750 benefit	£	150
Share of talent money for First or Second Division championship victory (total of £550 to share out), say	£	30
Bonus for League wins and draws throughout the season, worked on a rough average of 55 points for a championship victory at £1 a point	£	55
Share of talent money for winning the F.A. Cup (total of £550 to share out), say	£	30
Bonus for outright Cup victories in each round from the Third to the Final ...	£	55

Plus 10 per cent (all tax free) of all income

from a club to be paid on his retirement and which continues to the age of 35 if still playing ... ... £ 91

Rough estimate of eight internationals a year at £20 a match ... ... £ 160

Other payments or bonuses for such matches as Inter League, minor Cup-ties, etc. ... ... £ 39

Total per annum £1,200

That total is, of course, exceptional. For instance, it is scarcely likely for a club to win a First or Second Division championship and get to the final of the Cup the same year. But players with a good team can very easily earn £1,000 a year without winning a championship or getting to a Cup final. A fair average would be £18 to £20 a week, and no professional with any League club, whether 17-years-old or a part-timer, can earn less than £3 a week. **Minimum wage** for a full-time player aged 20 years and over is £7 a week in the playing season and £5 a week in the close season.

Here, it may be opportune to tell the story of the two footballers who were being re-signed for the following season. Number One went into the manager's office and eventually came out to tell Number Two that he had got £12 a week for the playing season and £10 a week for the close season.

Number Two then went in to see the manager and was offered £10 and £8.

" Why," said Number Two, " you've given £12 and £10 to Number One!"

" Yes, I know," said the manager in an effort to assuage his man, " but you see, he is a — well — a slightly better player than you. . . . "

" But not in the close season!" expostulated Number Two.

What may be termed the rank and file footballer, of course, draws less than his more talented or luckier colleague, but he doesn't starve, as that £7 and £5 minimum proves. He also qualifies **pro rata** for that additional tax free 10 per cent of income when he retires (this started at the beginning of the 1949-50 season, when the League clubs began paying into a common fund four per cent of their gates each week).

There is, of course, the question of the part-timer, but his case is best left until the "extras" a player can earn outside the game are discussed.

Work Two Hours a Day.

There are many footballers who do no more than train from 10 a.m. to noon from Monday to Friday, play one and a half hours on Saturday afternoon (more often in holiday periods, of course), and perhaps turn up at the ground on Sunday morning for a little massage.

Part of that two hours a day is also spent either on the massage table, or in front of the infra-red or ultra-violet ray lamps. It is also true to say that there is a fair amount of time spent in travelling mostly every other week-end—invariably in special coaches, rail or bus.

There are clubs, of course, who insist that players stay for lunch (which they may or may not pay for out of their own pockets) in order to put in a little more work, say, on lectures and other things in the afternoon. Maybe they will be taken to watch a League, Cup, or International match.

For some footballers, it is boring to have to turn up morning by morning for training, and doubly so if they have to stay on to four o'clock in the afternoon. That is when a few really begin to feel hardworked. . . .

Conversely, there are the conscientious souls who cannot do enough, or who have the sense to realize that playing in a match ought to be the easiest part of a week's work. There is the case of a footballer who was dropped because of poor form, but to save his feelings, the reason given to the Press was that he was suffering from a touch of influenza.

"If I'm suffering from 'flu," he is alleged to have said, "then I needn't turn up for training—only to collect my pay packet on Friday morning!" And according to the story, he didn't turn up at the ground until Friday morning. It never struck the poor sap that the longer he did that sort of thing, the longer he would stay out of the team—not until he was told.

Be Entertained Practically Every Other Week-end At Your Firm's Expense.

A footballer hasn't even to trouble his head about giving a waitress sixpence—it is all done for him. He stays in the best hotels, and often enjoys the luxury of a special lounge or dining room set specially aside for the party. Often a fellow coming from a poor-class home is bemused by such lavishness and doesn't like this life which his managers (or more particularly his directors) plan for him. Usually, he would prefer something more simple, but he gets used to it.

Spend a Fortnight Nearly Every Year on a Tour Abroad at the Firm's or Someone Else's Expense.

More and more clubs are making tours abroad, and the F.A.'s close-season plans are more ambitious than ever. Rio de Janeiro . . . Canada . . . America . . . South Africa . . . the Continent . . . the Mediterranean . . . the whole World is now opened up to the footballer

Matt Busby and Manchester United players discuss tactics on a table-top. Here, the famous manager makes the move which may win the next match. He is surrounded by such outstanding players as Johnny Carey, Allenby Chilton, Stanley Pearson, Johnny Aston and Henry Cockburn.

Photo: Sporting Chronicle.

First - class hotels, travel (mostly by air now), and expenses (sometimes £1 a day in addition to normal salary). What more could you wish for? It's better than joining the army!

Marvellous experiences, new places, new peoples, but the increasing responsibility of maintaining British prestige abroad—and playing up to it. It has its drawbacks—but not many. When Frank Swift retired, he thanked most people in football authority for " educating " him and giving him such a wonderful time. Home-loving footballers are torn when it comes to leaving their wives and families behind when they are lucky enough to be chosen for a tour, but it is an experience which they know is given to few people to the same extent.

There are more foreign tours than ever before, and for International players it is almost a duty, though they can refuse if they like — there has been a case of a notable player who had to refuse an F.A. tour because he was not a good traveller by air.

It is said that travel is an education. Well, the footballer of to-day is getting plenty of that.

Three Months' Summer Holidays.

May, June, and July are virtually " free " for the foot-baller to do as he pleases—a time of rest, because although his hours may be short, it is physically impossible for a man to be tuned-up for twelve months of the year. Maybe some of this time will be eaten into by tours, but on the whole he can devote himself to improving his business interests, resting, or, in the case of some men, playing cricket.

Many men put on weight alarmingly during this lay-off period and have quite a time getting it off when they turn up for training for a new season. On the whole, however, the footballer of to-day has a

C

ready appreciation of what is required of him, especially as his own future is involved by it. If he hasn't, then he is a fool.

Rent a Fully-furnished £1,500 House (and better) at 25s. a Week.

As now generally known, a married footballer has come to expect a club to find a house for him at a reasonable rent, and some even expect it to be furnished at 25s. a week! Some are more fortunate than others—some have to pay more than that, some don't get the furnishings. It all depends upon a footballer's luck, skill—and bargaining ability. For the single players, of course, it is a question of homely " digs," special club hostels, or, if he is lucky enough, the home in which he was brought up. It is a fact, however, that there are very few top-rank bachelor footballers.

Receive Various Free Meals and Entertainment.

Very often, clubs, especially during the Cup period or at crucial times in the League programme, will order special meals as part of a training programme, but it is not intended to lay undue stress on that. As for entertainment, the best seats are usually booked at a theatre where an away match is to be played and an overnight stay is entailed. That is a general policy— there are many invitations, especially to the top-class men, and it is true that the number of them can become most embarrassing, as Billy Wright has already indicated by saying that he will have to cut out many of them.

The Christmas Turkey.

Among the more influential clubs, this is quite an event, but there are few clubs who do not try to do something for their playing staff at Christmas in the shape of some permissible gift or other. It is a system which the footballer has come to accept as part of the goodwill between club and player.

WELL, that is generally the set-up of a footballer's life during his playing career, which reaches its height during his twenties and begins to taper off after he has turned thirty, until by the time he has reached thirty-five he is virtually finished. And it is that time which the player has constantly in mind, and about which, comment cannot be ignored.

In outlining the benefits which a footballer can get from the game while he is still capable, it is not intended to belittle him—only to throw an unbiassed light on his lot. The best get the best—the lesser-known ones have a harder struggle, though there are many men who would prefer to be a part-time player in the Third Division than a full-time one in the First.

Just one word is the reason for that—Security; security not only in the present, but in the future. . . . Something which will ensure a living whether he has to give up the game for one reason or another.

It is because of security that the Players' Union, the Football League, and the Football Association (in their joint standing committee) have worked together on the scheme which, introduced in 1949, will ensure a player of some form of nest-egg when he retires.

That is the social security scheme, already briefly outlined, into which the League clubs started paying from the start of the 1949-50 season four per cent of their gate receipts into a common fund which will ensure for a player ten per cent above every other known form of earnings he has gained from a League club or clubs when he retires.

That extra ten per cent of earnings goes on until player reaches 35—or sooner if he retires before then —in order to make some sort of provision for the time when he gives up the game.

Then there are the business and trade courses which are now conducted under the F.A. Scheme—sports, outfitting, engineering, accountancy, and so on, according to the inclination of a player. All this is designed to equip the footballer for the time when he retires.

There are some footballers who have become successful and rich business men without any help of this kind but through their own perspicacity and acumen. There are others who have been complete failures once football has been taken from them. That's what every footballer to-day is afraid of, and that is why he wants safeguards.

BLUE-PRINT FOR PLEASURE

An illegal pastime becomes
the sport of the million.

THERE are few games or sports which have not taken centuries to evolve. Soccer is one of them. When primordial man first became conscious that he could use his feet to kick an object, football was born. As his intelligence developed, so must his awareness of pain be increased until the prehistoric boulder was supplanted by the slain head of an enemy or something softer to kick around—with diminishing roars of anguish on his part and increasing roars of delight by the palæolithic spectator from his or her seat on a nearby cliff top (a rolled-up bearskin being easier to tolerate behind the ear than a rock thrown by an indignant player!).

Unfortunately, there are no tablets giving details of those early efforts—the hammer-and-chisel newspaper system of those days must have kept prehistoric poolsters waiting weeks in agony before they knew the results of three draws. We can, however, trace that over the centuries a form of football was evolved which embraced the whole of villages or factions, who played each other on certain festive occasions with the whole countryside—rivers, ravines, and all— as its pitch. That form of football, still robust but less fearsome, may be seen even to-day at Ashbourne, Derbyshire, on Shrove Tuesdays.

Rough rules embraced the forcing of the ball, bladder, or leather casing filled with cork to a certain stipulated point by the best—and worst—means possible. Free fights were common and broken limbs commonplace—refereeing demanded even greater courage, discretion, and speed than it does to-day!

The simple act of kicking something around became so popular that "the playeing of the futebal" was forbidden in the reign of Edward II "owing to the evil that might arise through so many people hustling together," and was also frowned upon by Richard II because he thought it interfered with the more serious pursuit of archery. There have been varying efforts since then to discourage the game, but it was like trying to order back the sea. "The futebal" just rolled on until it became so popular at the public schools that it was in those secluded cloisters that the first real foundations of the game as we know it to-day were laid.

It was certainly played at Westminster School at least two hundred and fifty years ago. Eton, Harrow, Rugby, Shrewsbury, Winchester, Charterhouse, Uppingham, and others all had their different forms or various interpretations of football, depending upon inclination or space. For instance, because of their good facilities, it became part of the game at Rugby to carry and throw the ball, and even for boys to be hurled around on the turf; at other schools, the cramped conditions compelled an advanced form of dribbling to develop.

It was only natural that as the boys left school they should seek means for continuing to play the game, and there were other young men too, who delighted in it as a recreation. Clubs were formed but many of them still had their own particular brand of football and finally an effort was made to clarify the situation. The London clubs convened a meeting on October 26, 1863, and decided to form a body called the Football Association—yes, the one we know to-day —but out of the meeting a split occurred.

A dispute arose as to whether the rules should allow a player to run and carry the ball and an opponent to trip him, and the camp became divided. On December 8, 1863, the F.A. decided to adopt the rules which largely made association football the game it is to-day, but Blackheath led a breakaway and helped to found the Rugby Union in 1871. It is interesting to reflect, therefore, that the Football Association is older than the Rugby Union by eight years and under its influence, soccer has made greater strides throughout the world than rugger.

The Scottish F.A. was formed in 1873, the Welsh F.A. in 1876, the Irish F.A. in 1880, the International Board (which governs the whole of British Soccer) in 1882, and the Federation Internationale de Football Associations (F.I.F.A.), which now governs the game throughout the world mainly by British influence, in 1904. Britain left F.I.F.A. in 1928 because it did not agree with certain things, but there was reconciliation at the end of the last war. The rest of the world could not really do without the long experience and sportsmanship of Britain, and we on our part thought it desirable to regain a say in the world development of the game.

For a moment let us flick back the pages of history briefly to pause on the names of three history-making clubs—Sheffield, formed in 1855, whose players were supposed to have played with half-crowns in each hand to make them resist the temptation of handling the ball; Notts County, the oldest in the Football League; and Queen's Park, the Glasgow amateurs, who, six years older than the Scottish F.A., were one of the original 15 clubs who played in the Football Association Challenge Cup.

The Cup, which gave the first great fillip to the game in a national sense, was introduced in 1871 and was won by the Wanderers, who beat the Royal Engineers in the first final, played at Kennington Oval, by the only goal of the match. They won it again the second year, when they beat Oxford University 2-0 at Lillie Bridge. Altogether, the Wanderers captured the Cup five times in the first seven competitions, the last three on consecutive occasions. By that feat they could have made the Cup their own property, but gave it back to the parent body on condition that it was to be a challenge trophy in perpetuity. The only other club to equal that hat-trick is Blackburn Rovers, who won in the years from 1884-86.

In point of fact, the F.A. Challenge Cup we know to-day is the third trophy. The original had been won by Aston Villa 1895 and was on view in a Birmingham tradesman's window when it was stolen, never to be seen again. That Cup had cost only £20, but it was not so much its intrinsic value as the glamour with which it has become surrounded that matters.

There are many more handsome trophies in the game to-day, even for junior competitions, but there's nothing like T'Owd Tin Pot, as they sometimes affectionately and humorously refer to it in Lancashire. There is warmth and deep feeling about that reference which shows just how much the whole country is endeared to the Cup and what it means, even though its plinth and lid do cause trouble to the winning captain each year as he receives it from the King.

The F.A. were pressed to provide a more magnificent trophy made of gold after the first one disappeared, but out of sentiment it was decided to make an exact replica of the original. The names of the previous winners were perpetuated on the second Cup, which was first won by Sheffield Wednesday, and which in February, 1911, was presented to Lord Kinnaird who, as the Hon. A. F. Kinnaird, had been a member of the Wanderers team when they won in 1873, 1877, and 1876, and the Old Etonians when they were successful in 1879 and 1882. He afterwards became president of the F.A. First winners of the third Cup (the present one) were Bradford City.

A year after the start of the F.A. Cup competition in 1871, official Internationals began. In those days, there were two half-backs and six forwards, two of them being centre-forwards, one of whom played just behind the other, and from which the centre half evolves. Shinguards came in 1874 and the crossbar was officially introduced the following year—a piece of tape had sometimes been stretched across from the top of the slender posts.

After the introduction of the F.A. Cup, which was followed within nine years by similar competitions in Scotland, Wales, and Ireland, the next two important steps were the legalisation of professionalism in 1885 and the formation of the Football League in 1888.

Lancashire became a stronghold of the game through the original influence of the little village of Turton, between Blackburn and Bolton. A club was established in 1872.

Before then, however, there was a series of scratch matches under Harrow rules, which combined Soccer and Rugger, thanks to the influence of the son of the lord of the manor, J. C. Kay, who came down from Harrow, and the village schoolmaster, W. T. Dixon. Mr. Kay used to take lanterns into the village on moonlight nights and he and a Mr. W. Forrest picked sides from the village lads, and whenever Mr. Kay's side won, each player was treated to drinks. The Kay's won consistently! Mr. Kay and Mr. Dixon eventually called a meeting in the Turton school and a club was formed with a membership fee of 1s. a head. There were eventually 48 members, and several times the team contained members all of whom lived in the same street. In 1874, Turton decided to embrace " London rules " and under the influence of that little village team, new clubs sprang up in Blackburn, Bolton, Darwen, and other places, and out of it, the Lancashire F.A. was formed.

Turton became members of the F.A. in 1876 and four years later their captain was J. J. Bentley, who eventually became chairman of Bolton Wanderers, one of the founders and president of the Football League, and a vice-president of the F.A. With the coming of "shamateurism" and the eventual recognition of professionalism, however, little Turton, like so many others of their kind, could not compete against clubs in the big centres and eventually died out in 1910.

Meanwhile, clubs began to cast round in wider circles for players and although he may not actually have been the first professional, Fergie Suter was regarded as one of those who helped to start a fashion which has now become an institution. He appeared in a Partick team which was beaten by Blackburn Rovers in 1878. Shortly afterwards, he went to Darwen, ostensibly as a stonemason. He had a greater penchant for playing football, however, and though he did appear regularly for Darwen, he left there in 1880 and became a Blackburn player. The same year, Jimmy Douglas joined Rovers from Renfrew— Hughie McIntyre, formerly captain of Glasgow Rangers, had gone there the previous year, and another ex-Ranger in Peter Campbell followed the three of them.

It was not believed that those Scotsmen went to Blackburn solely for their health, a fact which was duly noted by Rovers' nearby rivals, Preston North End, and the Football Association moved in the matter so that in 1885 professionalism was officially recognised. It was one of the most sensible things that could have happened.

Now the stage was set for the next important step —the institution of the Football League. Just three years after the recognition of professionalism, the Football League was founded under its "father," Mr.

William McGregor. The game cried out for such a move. Until then, it had been played week by week in local leagues, mostly on the county pattern. Only the Cup competition was national.

So the Football League came into being, with its headquarters in Preston, where they have been ever since. At first, there were only 12 clubs—six from Lancashire (Accrington, Blackburn Rovers, Bolton Wanderers, Burnley, Everton, and Preston North End) and the other half-dozen mostly from the Midlands (Aston Villa, Derby County, Notts County, Stoke, West Bromwich Albion, and Wolverhampton Wanderers).

Those clubs played the following season, but in 1890-91, Stoke dropped out and Sunderland came in. A year later, the League was increased to 14 clubs when Stoke came back and Darwen joined in. That was the time when the penalty kick was first introduced. In 1892-3, it grew to 16, and the Second Division was formed. The Darwen club never seemed properly to be able to make up its mind. It went out, and although Small Heath, Nottingham Forest, and Sheffield Wednesday were only too pleased to take their chance, Darwen reappeared with yet another new club, Sheffield United, the following year, when Accrington and Notts County then temporarily disappeared.

Liverpool came in in 1894-95, surrendered their place in the First Division to Bury the following season, but returned in 1896-97.

So it went on until, ten years after the formation of the League, clear-cut promotion and relegation was introduced. Upon the formation of the Second Division in 1892, a series of test matches were played between the bottom two in the First Division and the top two in the Second to decide which two should be included among the 16 senior clubs.

Stoke, Burnley, Newcastle United, and Blackburn Rovers were the last four clubs to play in these test matches. Stoke needed a point from their last game with Burnley, who themselves required only the same thing for promotion.

The match turned out to be a draw, but it was such a pantomime—so many balls were kicked into the crowd, who retained them—that five had to be used altogether. The coincidence was too much for the authorities, and so automatic promotion and relegation came in, but upon Burnley's successful proposal that the First and Second Divisions be each extended, Blackburn retained their place, and Newcastle got theirs by election.

So did the game go through various processes, the "colour" of which is apt to be missed in a short history of this kind. However, the First Division was extended to 20 clubs in 1905-6, and in 1919-20 there division. The Third Division South was formed the following year, and the Northern Section the year after.

Meanwhile, between the formation of the Football League in 1888 and the build-up to its form in 1921 the game experienced many things. Here are a few:—

Goal nets were introduced in 1891 to clear up the disputes which occurred about scoring; Preston North End (1888-89) and Aston Villa (1896-97) became the only two clubs in the history of the game to win both the Cup and League championship in the same season; a maximum wage rule came into force (1901); the first £1,000 transfer came in when Middlesbrough paid Sunderland that sum for centre-forward Alf Common (1905); a transfer limit of £350 was fixed in January, 1908, but was withdrawn in April (how the clubs do seem constantly to have made a rod for their own backs); the Scottish Cup was withheld owing to a riot after two drawn games between Rangers and Celtic at Hampden Park in 1909; King George V, the first reigning monarch to do so, attended the Cup Final between Burnley and Liverpool in 1914, and Entertainment Tax was introduced in 1916.

The game received terrific impetus following the first World War, just as it has done after the second one. After 1921, highlights have been:

1922: The Corinthians, the last of the great amateur teams to hold their own against professionals, but now forced into mediocrity, entered the F.A. Cup.

1923: The first Wembley Cup Final, or the White Horse Final as it became known because of the mounted policeman who patrolled the touchlines to keep back the crowd, many of whom had broken in, was won by the Bolton Wanderers against West Ham United.

1925: The offside law was changed from three men to two men in front of the man receiving the ball. Billy McCracken, the old Newcastle United full-back was supposed to be the man mainly responsible for the change because of the manner in which he ran up the field to put forwards offside, a lead that was followed by other defenders to such an extent that stoppages became exasperating. From the change in the offside law the stopper centre half originated.

1926: Huddersfield Town became the first club to win the League championship three times in succession—a hat-trick which was equalled by Arsenal in 1935.

1927: The F.A. Cup was taken out of England for the first time—by Cardiff City.

1928: Herbert Chapman, who laid the foundation for both the Huddersfield and Arsenal triumphs, became the first manager in the game to pay £10,000 for a player when, as manager of Arsenal, he signed David Jack famous inside right, from Bolton Wanderers.

1934: An official trial was given to the idea of having two referees in a match—it was considered in some quarters that the game had got beyond the control of one referee.

1936: Jimmy McGrory (Glasgow Celtic) set up a new British scoring record of 386 goals solely in Scottish League football, but increased it to 410 by the time of his retirement in 1938, and altogether scored 550 goals in recognised first-class football. Hughie Gallacher (Airdrie, Newcastle, and Chelsea) scored 386 League goals, " Dixie " Dean (Tranmere Rovers, Everton, and Notts County), 379; Hugh Ferguson (Motherwell and Cardiff City), 362; and Steve Bloomer (Derby County), 352.

1937: Biggest official crowd at any British match 149,547 at the Scotland v. England International at Hampden Park (it was believed that there were 150,000 at the first Wembley final, although it was impossible to estimate accurately the number because of the break-in).

1938: As they had done in Herbert Chapman's day, Arsenal again set up a world record by paying the highest transfer fee of £14,000 for Bryn Jones, from Wolverhampton Wanderers. That was the biggest fee ever paid for a player before the Second World War.

1939: Numbering of players officially introduced; watering of pitches regulated so that hoses are not used in November, December, January, and February, and the first six-figure attendance (118,567) at a League match—Rangers v. Celtic (record for a League match in England is the 82,950 at the Manchester United-Arsenal game at Maine Road, Manchester, in January, 1948).

1946: Longest official match ever played—203 minutes. It was a Third Division North Cup-tie between Stockport County and Doncaster Rovers, when wartime conditions still compelled the playing of cup-ties until a definite decision was reached. However, spectators went home for tea and returned in time to see the players still battling away when bad light stopped play at 6.43 p.m. with both sides at 4-4!

1947: Great Britain beat the Rest of Europe (captained by United's Eire-born Johnny Carey) 6-1 at Glasgow and Doncaster Rovers set up a new Football League record of 72 points in winning the Third Division North championship.

1949: Biggest-ever transfer—£25,000 for Johnny Morris when Derby County signed him from Manchester United.

1950: Transfer record beaten again—Preston North End pay Sheffield Wednesday £26,500 for Eddie Quigley, Johnny Morris' uncle!

WELL, that is a short history of the manner in which the game has come to the million or more spectators who watch Soccer week by week. There are still great things being done and still greater things to be done.

No sport since the introduction of horse-racing has captured the imagination of the peoples of the earth more than this one. Most people are surprised that it has not become more popular in the United States. It has movement and colour and mainly because of the increasing interest of the Latin peoples is likely to become faster and more thrilling even yet.

There is no one who can forecast where it will end.

THE BIRTH OF PROFESSIONALISM

An act which
" democratised " the sport.

A BRIEF reference has already been made to the manner in which professionalism was legalised, but the subject demands more attention than that, because it was one of the important things which helped to send the game hurrying hotfoot round the world. It brought tremendous problems in those early days and they have persisted ever since, but there is no one who can deny that the game has advanced beyond all original conceptions under the influence of the paid player.

The similarity between the problems of to-day and over sixty years ago is remarkable. It is said that there is nothing new under the sun, and here is a case to prove it. The problem of under-the-counter payments is older than the Football League itself.

What professionalism did was to thrust amateurism largely in the background in popular public appeal, and even though the old spirit is retained as far as possible, it is a fact that no amateur club has won the Cup since Old Etonians beat Blackburn Rovers in 1882.

The early influences, of course, were all-amateur, but the first rumblings of professionalism came around 1877 when Peter Andrews and James J. Lang, who had both gained Scottish caps, went to Sheffield and joined the old Heeley club. That was followed by the appearance of Fergus Suter and James Love in the Darwen " team of working lads " who reached the fourth round of the Cup in 1879, only to be beaten by Old Etonians. It has never been admitted that these four Scotsmen were actually professionals with Heeley or Darwen, but at least it was said that they started a trek over the border for the " siller " which was to be found in England, whether from football or not. Whatever it was, these Scotsmen brought a style which appealed to the public and inspired their English team-mates. Until the Scottish system of the studious pass and close combination was introduced, the long dribble was quite a feature of the English game.

Around the same time, a Shropshire business magnate offered gold watches to the local team if they won the Cup, and what with American and Canadian trips hinted at for Scotland and Darwen, the old order was beginning to disappear. So much so, that in referring to a dispute between Darwen and Blackburn Rovers, in which he credited the latter with unsportsmanlike behaviour, the hon. secretary of the F.A. at that time, Mr. C. W. Alcock, a man of strong amateur tendencies —he was a member of Wanderers' first Cup-winning team—but wide vision, said:—" There is no use to disguise the speedy approach of a time when the subject of professional players will require the earnest attention of those on whom devolves the management of Association Football."

That time was, indeed, rapidly approaching. From a trickle, the Scots were pouring over the border in a flood and all sorts of tales were told of officials who paid openly and were ready to stand the consequences; of others who " cooked " the gates, and of players who unexpectedly found money in their pockets.

All this could not be ignored and in 1881 the F.A. passed a rule with a huge hole in it. It admitted broken-time payments for time lost at work in playing football. Otherwise, players breaking the rule were to be debarred from the Cup, Inter-Association, and International matches, and any club transgressing debarred from membership of the Association.

D

It was stated at the time that if the ruling authority had taken a firm stand they could have stamped out professionalism, but that view cannot seriously be accepted in the light of events. The effect, at least, was to clear the consciences for the time being of people who were in favour of the paid player.

The situation was not completely satisfactory, however, and even such centres as Sheffield and Birmingham had not outwardly gone to the lengths of certain Lancashire clubs, and questions about the number of Scotsmen Blackburn Rovers played were openly asked.

What was most important, however, was that the game was spreading rapidly, amateurism or professionalism notwithstanding, and despite the fact that in the provinces the Rugby code was highly popular, albeit less organized. Blackburn Rovers became the first Northern club to reach the final of the Cup—in 1882, when they were beaten by Old Etonians, and the following year, Blackburn Olympic became the first Northern team to win the trophy (it did not go South again until nineteen years later, by which time professionalism had been clearly established).

Preston North End, or its benefactor, Mr. W. Sudell, can claim to have brought the professional problem clearly to a head. Preston started as a Rugby club in 1877, but inspired by the performances of Darwen and Blackburn, adopted the Association rules. Rovers beat North End 16-0 in an exhibition game in 1881. and this, allied to other heavy defeats Preston had suffered, caused Mr. Sudell to ponder the best means of placing his club in the forefront. He could not fail to note the number of Scotsmen Blackburn played, and he followed the lead, backed up by his associates. " Employment " was soon found for J. Belger, from Glasgow; " Nick " Ross, great back and captain of Midlothian, and G. Drummond, A. S. Robertson,

Davie Russell, John Graham, " Jimmy " Ross, and Sam Thompson. Two local youths R. H. Howarth and R. Holmes, showed great ability, and thus a new side was formed almost in a season. Other clubs were not slow to note all this, and at one time, Bolton Wanderers had only one Englishman in their first eleven.

Mr. Sudell refused to be discouraged by the suspension of Accrington and the disqualification of three players, Jones (Walsall) and Hidgetts and Green (St. George's) by the Birmingham Association, and Preston were disqualified from the Cup after drawing with Upton Park in the first round of the second series in January, 1884.

At the inquiry, Mr. Sudell was so frank that he must have shocked some of the legislators at the time. He openly admitted payment to players, but urged that the practice was common. This admission led to a quickening of effort on the part of the sub-committee which had been set up to investigate the subject of importations and payments. It moved a resolution, proposed by Mr. Alcock (who was also secretary of the Surrey County Cricket Club), at the annual general meeting of the Association : " That professionalism be legalised, the details to be submitted to a subsequent special general meeting of the Association."

It is believed that Mr. Alcock had in mind the happy relationship which already existed in cricket between the paid and unpaid player, but there is no doubt that he had primarily at heart the important aim of maintaining the Football Association as the paramount authority over the game in all its aspects. An unpaid official himself, his broad-mindedness and foresight were remarkable.

Still the general meeting would not accept the inevitable. It was swayed by the strong views of the

Sheffield and Birmingham Associations on the " evils " of professionalism, and as a result, the Association attempted to strengthen its rules for repressive action. It is noteworthy that Mr. J. C. Clegg—who became chairman of the F.A. Council—was one of those wholeheartedly against professionalism. He had been a famous amateur runner.

A special committee drew up a scheme to call on clubs charged with offences to prove their innocence, and books, letters, and other necessary documents could be inspected if necessary. The lost wages clause was narrowed so that it applied to only one day in any week; only English-born players with English clubs in Association Cup-ties was another stipulation, and coupled with all this, it was required of clubs that they make returns of imported players, their occupations and wages prior to and after their moves, and reasons for such changes.

This naturally led to a still further stiffening of attitude on the part of those clubs who favoured professionalism until they were on the verge of revolt. On October 15, 1884, a meeting of 19 clubs, mostly from Lancashire, was held at Blackburn, and it was decided to form a new body called the British Football Association, rather than give up the principle of importations and payments.

Shortly afterwards, another meeting was held in Manchester; this time 31 clubs were represented, and steps were taken to form a constitution and get the new association going. However, the Lancashire Association, which would have been the first to suffer from such an open rupture, agitated for some less drastic method of dealing with the situation. It was at least made plain to the committee of the F.A. dealing with the whole thing that any hope of driving out professionalism could be considered at an end.

The fight was not over yet by a long way, however.

Birmingham were still uncompromising. Yet the Southern amateur representatives—and this is most surprising—took no narrow view of the situation.

Next move was the appointment by the F.A. of a representative sub-committee who met in Manchester in November, 1884, when Mr. Alcock proposed: "That it is expedient to legalise professionalism under stringent conditions."

This was reported back to the Association committee, who adopted it by thirteen votes to five, ten of the thirteen being Southerners. Altogether, there were nine resolutions, the substance of which was:—

(a) Professionals were allowed to play under the auspices of the Association so long as they had a birth qualification within twelve miles of the club's headquarters, or two years' residence;

(b) Professionals were debarred from any active part in legislation, and

(c) Competitions for prizes not offered by a club or Association forbidden unless the proceeds went to some club or charity.

The proposals went before a special general meeting of the Association the following January and were again defeated. Mr. Alcock then moved the legalisation of professionals under stringent conditions, to which Mr. C. Crump, of the Birmingham Association moved an amendment seconded by Mr. Chambers, of the Sheffield Association "That the introduction of professionalism will be the ruin of the pastime and it is most unwise to permit it."

Now, Preston's Mr. Sudell entered the scene again by declaring that he could prove that professionalism existed in Birmingham and Sheffield to an extent that probably its opponents were not aware. Then Mr. W. McGregor, of the Aston Villa club, who three years later was to become the "father" of the Football League, stood up to favour legalisation of the paid player. A vote was taken and there were 113 for and 108 against the introduction of outright professionalism, but it was lost on the two-thirds majority rule of the Association.

Not a thing was carried—not even repressive proposals; it was a deadlock and a definite split became imminent. Those who wanted the paid player kept their rival association. Again the question was raised and lost on the two-thirds majority rule at the annual general meeting in March, 1885, but at a special general meeting in the following July, the battle ended. The case for recognised professionals was won.

There were fewer than fifty representatives present at that last fateful gathering, thirty-five voting in favour of Dr. Morley's proposal that the recommen tion of the committee be adopted and five against. The rules which were then added for the opening of the 1885-86 season are historical:—

" Professionals shall be allowed to compete in all Cups, County, and Inter-Association matches, provided they be qualified as follows:—

" (a)   In Cup matches by birth or residence for two years last past within six miles of the ground or headquarters of the Club for which they play.

" (b)   In County matches as defined in Rule XI, which applies equally to all players whether amateur or professional.

" (c)   In Inter-Association matches by **bona fide** membership for two years last past of some Club belonging to one of the competing Associations.

" No professional shall be allowed to serve on any Association Committee or represent his own or any other Club at any meeting of the Football Association.

" No professional shall be allowed to play for more than one club in any one season without special permission of the Committee of the Football Association.

"All professionals shall be annually registered in a book to be kept by the Committee of the Football Association, and no professional shall be allowed to play unless he has been registered."

The pattern closely followed that which existed in County Cricket. For instance, the Rule XI referred to stated " That in County matches the qualifications required be those recognised by the leading County Cricket Clubs."

The football family thus became re-united, but some bitterness still remained in Birmingham, Sheffield, and Nottingham, though even that was removed by the passage of years. The game had got over one of its biggest obstacles.

Before this chapter is closed, however, there is another aspect which needs ventilation. The Scottish Association, which had come to terms with the Football Association on the question of playing rules, was naturally perturbed at the exodous of their players and did something about it. They drew up a list of sixty-eight men who had gone to English clubs and forbade them from playing in Scotland again without special permission. They were so bitter, in fact, that for several years they played only amateurs in their International games, whereas England were not averse to including men of " doubtful " status if they justified their places.

MANAGERS AND THEIR METHODS

Herbert Chapman gives an
old game a new kick.

WHEN Alex James was once asked why he did not
take up the managership of a club, he replied: " Why
should I give myself stomach ulcers?"

In one expressive sentence, Alex had pin-pointed
just what it means to be a manager, with the worries,
fears, hopes, disappointments, restlessness and occasional glory which the job entails. A manager can
be at the top one minute and be kicked out the next.

Think, for instance, of the man whose team won
the Cup one year, the First Division Championship
the next, and two seasons later slumped into the
Second Division for no very apparent reason.

The scapegoat is invariably the manager. No one
can regard himself as safe in the position. Even
when he is basking in the praise of some splendid
achievement, there is always the shadow of what next
might happen. An unwanted situation can erupt as
suddenly as Vesuvius and smash the planning of years.

The big buy can easily turn out to be the false buy
—what was the manager thinking of? There is always
to-morrow of which to think—of the youngster who, it
is hoped, will be good enough to take the place of the
" star " player now reaching the end of his career; or
the fresh honour to be won and the fresh challenge
to come.

The manager must meet demands from six major
sources—legislators, directors, players, public, rival
clubs, and the press. There never is the perfect state,
and the best player does not always make the best
manager—there have been many notable failures.

Managers must possess tact, charm, cunning, generalship, vision, patience, courage, and a heap of other things. Yes, Alex James was right when he mentioned those ulcers, but this chapter is not meant to pity the manager—only to praise him, or such of them who have made remarkable contributions to the game during the last few tumultuous decades of soccer.

In that time, the game has been lifted from wooden hoardings and corrugated iron to vast new stadia of steel and concrete; from simple methods to advanced tactical skill; from the effects of two World Wars to peace-time efficiency—and with it all, the growth of counter-attractions and the challenge from abroad.

It is a fact that after each World War came remarkable evolutions in managership; it was as though hostilities in each case brought out deeper-thinking men. The reality of war seemed to be translated into the reality of peace—the millions of people who had been uprooted by war did not want to go back to the old ideas.

So far as Soccer is concerned, the men have always been produced for the occasion. Old-timers cannot tolerate present-day standards, but who or which is right? Can those million or more spectators a week all be wrong? Ask the managers. Take the view of one of the latest bosses—Horatio Carter, who says: "There is nothing seriously wrong with the game on the whole. What the older enthusiast forgets is that a new generation has arisen, a generation which never knew the old methods, and which may positively dislike them if they were re-presented now." And Carter, one of England's wonder inside forwards with Sunderland and Derby County, and player-manager of the phenomenal Hull City, is the very epitome of the new age, the new-type manager. He demonstrates the change from managers in mufti to managers in track suits—yes, and even in football kit, playing alongside the lads whose destiny he guides.

It is no disparagement to say that managers before the first World War were largely men of mature age who superintended their club from the office chair or a seat in the stands. They were, indeed, a remarkable body of men, some of whom achieved unqualified success. To many of them, blackboard tactics were unknown or too ridiculous for words.

There was, of course, keen competition even in those days, but not to the same marked degree as between the wars, which was less urgent than to-day. The tempo gets faster, and to-day is always urgent, whether it is this year or next.

So the conditions after the 1914-18 war, with its new influences, demanded men with fresh ideas, and into the scene stepped Herbert Chapman, who had been a forward of no marked ability with Grimsby Town, but who may go down in history as the greatest manager Soccer will ever have.

He had passed an examination to become a member of the Institute of Mining Engineers when he was persuaded to apply for the player-managership of Northampton Town, a position he secured; he then went to the old Leeds City club, thence to Huddersfield Town, and finally to Arsenal. He transformed the club and at the same time transformed soccer.

It is interesting to reflect, however, what his margin of success would have been had not the offside rule suddenly changed from three men in front of the player receiving the ball to the present two.

Bill McCracken, of Newcastle United fame, had, of course, set a fashion for full-backs in running up the field and putting opposing forwards offside. Such tactics caused so many hold-ups that it was decided to change the law and make it more difficult for defenders to work the offside trap.

At first, clubs stuck to the old attacking centre half-back, and the first reaction was a spate of goals

—the forwards got through too easily. Something had to be done about **that.** And something was done. The centre half stayed at home. He became the third-back, the stopper, the policeman. It is popularly supposed that Herbert Chapman originated the then new defensive system with Herbert Roberts & Co. but Charlie Spencer, present manager of Grimsby Town, claims that he was the first " stopper " centre half-back when he was playing with Newcastle. That is important, because here was a club, one of whose players (McCracken) had primarily led the way to a change in Soccer law, now finding a quick alternative to the alteration, whether they were the first or not.

But there is no doubt that if Chapman did not originate the third-back principle, he did perfect it to such an extent that he has been both praised and reviled. And he did it so well that Arsenal became the biggest power in club football.

Everyone talked about Arsenal, the club which had previously enjoyed nothing more than mediocrity. They won the Cup and the League and practically every other honour with monotonous regularity by their goal-snatching methods—three forwards up, a long clearance, a surprise raid, and back into solid defence.

Their success spread abroad. Continentals clamoured to see the Arsenal. Their colours and their methods were eagerly adopted. They had their " fans " all over the country—and still have. They also became the most despised club in the land—supporters of other clubs went into tantrums because their own team would batter long and hard at that defence and still not get through. Defence became a mania, and although there are distinct signs of greater attractiveness of play, the accent is still largely on the " stopper ", which has now become the easiest job on the field.

That is what Chapman did to football. He was a visionary—a planner. He gave the footballer a new status. He insisted upon men with character—it was said that he once sent a player home because he turned up for training wearing a muffler instead of a collar and tie; the "star" had to turn up at the right time for training as much as the young learner.

The blackboard and chess-like moves became an accepted part of the new training curriculum. He was the first man ever to pay £10,000 for a player (David Jack, now manager of Middlesbrough). He was the first manager properly to realise the value of press and other publicity. He said that if it were possible for him to return to the game as a player it would be at wing half-back and he would play for England—he regarded that position as the most important in a team.

Since Chapman, George Allison has been manager of Arsenal, and now it is Tom Whittaker, who in Chapman's day was trainer. It is obvious that the old master left a very big impression on the new one. Much of the well-known Arsenal policy is still followed, though the old established team methods are altered—with accent still on defence but more attractive ideas in attack.

Arsenal are now playing a type of football which was brought into emphasis when Cliff Britton (in charge at Everton, where he was once a player) was manager of Burnley during their Cup Final and promotion-winning year after the second World War.

Britton brought the whole of his players back into defence when the opposing team was on the attack, so that when Burnley took the ball up the field, they did so by the short pass from man to man. It ensured that the whole team moved with the ball, as distinct from the old Arsenal policy of the long clearance to one of three men lying upfield. It became known as the clockwork method. The ball moved tick-tock fashion.

There was no wild lashing at the ball, no fierce shooting. It was taken right up to the opposing goal-mouth and mainly slipped into the net. It gave solidity in defence and a certain amount of attractiveness in attack—not many goals were given away, and not many goals were scored.

Whittaker, with stronger forwards than Britton has yet been blessed with since he became a manager, has modified the style to his own liking and introduced a new move: his wingmen occasionally fall back and mark opposing wingmen. This was first seen most noticeably on the day that Ian McPherson marked the renowned Stanley Matthews—notice that it is still a defensive move, however, even though it could be turned into attack.

Have you noticed that very few players want to move from Arsenal? Bryn Jones, £14,000 player, was content for a long time to stay with the club if only as twelfth man. Joe Mercer has said that he never thought there could be a club so marvellous to its players as Arsenal. What a tribute in these days of accentuated player-restlessness! Praise the manager.

There are many who believe that Major Frank Buckley not only challenged Chapman, but in many respects led him in that between-the-wars period. Even to-day, Buckley, the man with the Midas touch, who claims that he has never yet left a club " in the red," is one of the most outstanding in managerial capacity.

Here is a man who staggered the football world with watered pitches, gland treatment for players, the selling of Bryn Jones for the pre-war record transfer fee, and, virtually, the nine-weeks revival of Hull City. This and much more has " The Major " achieved. It would not be derogative to call him " Blitz " Buckley —at times, he just blows convention sky-high.

Buckley was one of the first of the few—the successful player who turned out to be the highly successful manager. Manchester-born, he played as a half-back for Brighton and Hove, Aston Villa, both Manchester clubs, Birmingham, Derby County, Bradford City, and England.

He became a major in the Footballers' Battalion in the first World War, after which, he took up the managership of Norwich City, thence to Blackpool, and on to Wolverhampton Wanderers, where the real genius of the man became mainly evident. In the four-years' period from May, 1935, he revealed such an aptitude for finding and making young players, that Wolves "lifted" £110,000 in transfer fees alone. Buckley paid out £42,000 for players in the same period, so that the total favourable margin was £68,000. In addition, Wolves in the two years before the second World War were twice runners-up for the League Championship and Wembley Cup finalists with Portsmouth in 1939.

Here is a man who has never been loath to make the most daring experiments. He brought into League football lads of 17 and less. His most famous "find," of course, was Stan Cullis, who has taken over the managerial reins at Wolverhampton, but there have been many, many more. Frank Buckley's "discoveries" are legion.

He caused fierce controversy when he introduced gland treatment for his young Wolves players, but medical opinion found nothing wrong in it; he artificially flooded the ground at Molineux so much that he caused the Football League to introduce the present law about the watering of pitches—not now permissible during November, December, January, and February.

During the last war he went to Notts County, where his salary was supposed to be £4,000 a year, but soon left—not before selling Jesse Pye to Wolves, however (It has been said that " The Major " sold Pye because his own code of honour forbade him leaving a club without showing a profit).

Then on to Hull City, a club which had been revived after the war. Here a new site had been found and a new ground capable of holding over 40,000 erected in a few short weeks—Buckley himself formed his team in the nine weeks before the 1946-47 season opened. And that team reached the third round of the Cup, as it did the season afterwards, with further additions, of course.

During Buckley's short stay at Boothferry Park, Hull City narrowly failed to win promotion, and just after Horatio Carter had been signed as player-assist-ant-manager, " The Major " left to take over Leeds United, where he still is, and where he introduced yet another 17-years-old to League football in centre half-back John Charles, reckoned to be better than Stan Cullis was at the same age.

Throughout his managerial career, Buckley has moved to football centres with bigger populations. He has never been afraid to transfer men, and he has been just as bold in signing them. And in his first season with Leeds United, they had the biggest profit they have ever known. Yes, this is the manager with the Midas touch. . . .

Less flamboyant, but in his own way just as suc-cessful was Jack Tinn, of the famous spats and mem-orable philosophy: " Never forget the social side of football." A former county court official who had given much of his spare time to football, Tinn entered the managerial side of the game when South Shields were elected to the Second Division in 1919. A year later, Portsmouth was one of those who made up the new Third Division.

In 1927, therefore, Jack Tinn went to a Soccer outpost. He joined Portsmouth as manager, and though by that time they had won promotion to the First Division, they have never been out of it, and Tinn saw them to four Wembley Cup finals, three in peace-time (1929, 1934, and 1939, when they beat Wolves), and once in war-time.

It can truthfully be said that he raised the game in the country's Southernmost region to the level of that in the North, Midlands, and London. It was a re-markable achievement, and all of it was achieved with-out the surplus of money we know to-day.

Jack Tinn is now talent-spotting for Aston Villa. Since his departure, of course, Portsmouth have won the League Championship in their jubilee season under likeable, capable " Bob " Jackson, who, were he asked, would probably be the first to admit the pion-eering quality of the man who preceded him.

That between-the-wars period could bring in many famous managers—" Bob " Jack (father of David Jack), who did so much in another Soccer outpost, Plymouth; " Clem " Stephenson, a famous player who followed Herbert Chapman at Huddersfield; Dick Ray, another player who, when manager of Leeds United, became the first team manager ever appointed to take charge of a Football League representative team; Fred Everiss, of West Bromwich long service, who is reputed never to have had a partiality for Scottish players (unlike Preston chairman Mr. Jim Taylor), and so on. . . .

Now, we reach the era of new-type managers—Walter Winterbottom, Matt Busby, Cliff Britton, Horatio Carter, Stan Cullis, Peter Doherty, Freddie Steele, and even Ivor Broadis. When men discarded their battle-dress after the second World War, clubs began to look round for new managers, and what their eyes lighted upon mostly were famous players who had learned their coaching skills either in the Services' physical training schemes or under the F.A. plan.

Everton v. whom? At the height of the fight by the Football League against the pools in the mid-thirties, fixtures were withheld until the last moment and this is how clubs tried to advertise their matches.

Photo: Daily Dispatch.

The last stage of the journey of your pools coupon. A picture which provides a striking commentary on the manner in which the soccer pools industry has grown, shows girl clerks bundling up both winning and losing coupons. Afterwards, these are put in a safe place for reference if required.

Photo: Littlewoods, Liverpool.

Without doubt, Winterbottom and Busby have been the outstanding men of their kind in these post-war years. Winterbottom, former schoolmaster, Manchester United half-back, and squadron-leader on the R.A.F. physical training side during the war, holds a new post in the game—chief F.A. coach and England team manager. It has been a most successful appointment, and it could truthfully be said that he has been one of the main reasons why English International football has been so prominent since the last war, despite what happened at Rio.

Even yet, we have not reached pre-war perfection—but is perfection ever reached? Under these young managers, however, there are very definite signs of improvement, and in the individual case of Manchester United (under Matt Busby, of course), they have shown to every club the rewards which will justly go to those who constantly strive for perfection on the playing field.

Never at any time in the game has the blackboard played such an important part in tactics. All these managers to-day know just how important it is to dissect the faults of a match just played and the vital points about a team next to be met.

There is a greater and greater demand for that type of manager who goes out onto the practise field to play with his lads and show them exactly what he wants. Even that has been taken a stage further with player-managers like Carter, Doherty, and Steele. Naturally, these three cannot last forever as players, and furthermore, they cannot afford the time to go out into the highways and byways to watch players who may be badly needed for reinforcements. There are limitations to wearing football kit week by week, but the track suit looks as though it will remain part of a manager's equipment in the years ahead.

E

The name of Ivor Broadis, Sunderland inside forward, has been included in this discussion because his case is unique. Here is a man who did not give up his playing career to become a manager, but a man who gave up a managership to become a player—an International "cap" was the attraction. When Broadis was player-manager of Carlisle United, he was the youngest in the game to be in charge of a club. But he was also such a good player that finally he was tempted to give up (temporarily at least) the managerial side of his career.

That was because of his desire to play for England. So far, that has not yet been achieved. As player-manager of Carlisle, he had to negotiate his own transfer to Sunderland—he received offers from many clubs, and placed them before his board. Now, he is one of the successes of one of the most expensive forward lines in the country.

The game has its traditions, its thrills, its famous players and administrators—but where would it be without its managers?

INFLUENCE OF THE POOLS

The coupon drops through the
letter box and a new epoch begins.

EARLY in the 1930's a new influence arose—football
pools. Soccer became a means for making a fortune.
The old fixed odds methods, while still popular,
became of secondary importance. In the pools, the
masses found a modern El Dorado. From the
promiscuous " tanner " and " bob ", highly-systemised
methods developed until even the promoters, in an
effort to reduce the power of permutation syndicates,
placed a limit on the amounts staked on each coupon.

But although there have been varying attempts
to curb the influence of the pools, nothing has
prevented them from becoming a part of our weekly
existence. Not even the fact that some promoters
have made millions out of them unduly worries the
public: the appeal of placing a 1, 2, or X on a piece of
paper winning a life of luxury is far too great an
attraction.

From bath night, Friday has turned into pools night
—the most popular time of the week for filling in the
coupon, the time when whole families get together
and if father has not had any luck with all his know-
ledge, mother takes a turn just to see what she can
do. And generally, mother is just as fortunate as
father !

One of the clearest indications of what it all means
has been given by the Director General of the G.P.O.
in his evidence to the Royal Commission on Betting.
He said that football pools account for a turnover of
£600,000,000 a year, giving the G.P.O. one tenth of its
business and a profit of about £3,000,000 a year.

" We like this traffic very much," continued the Director General. " We charge the full amount (on postal orders, stamps, etc.), and it is easy to handle. If the pools were stopped, four hundred Post Office employees would be redundant and in the long run some one thousand people out of a hundred thousand employed on general postal work would be affected. Sixty per cent of postal orders sold are concerned with betting."

It is now reckoned that with Sir Stafford Cripps' extra taxation, the pools pay the Government £21,000,000 a year in tax, postage, and poundage. Even that does not seem to worry the public—even if the fortune-winning dreams are not realised this week, there is always a chance next week.

British football has turned out to be an admirable means for pools wagering. Despite any criticisms which may be made about such things as under-the-counter payments in effecting transfers of players and so on, there is not a sport of such magnitude in the world to-day which is run straighter or is better organized.

In view of this, Soccer has steadfastly refused to take a penny from the pools promoters, who from time to time have shown an honest eagerness to make some contribution to a sport which has earned them fortunes. That fight by the Football League against the pools in February, 1936, by withholding fixtures until the last minute is still a vivid memory. It was erroneously believed that the promoters would find the question of coupon-distribution so difficult that they would be forced out of business. In point of fact, the game itself was thrown into complete chaos and the fight had to be abandoned after three strenuous weeks. Here are the almost day-by-day facts :—

February 20 : Football League clubs meeting in Manchester decided not to proceed with any plan whereby the football pools and coupon firms would be required to make monetary contributions for the use of the League's fixtures, copyright in which, in the opinion of counsel, was established in the Football League. It was hinted that the League Management Committee, acting on the meeting's decision, would seek to prevent pools and coupon firms from using any Football League fixture-lists.

February 21 : Revealed that fixtures prepared for the remainder of the season were likely to be cancelled; that League clubs for the remainder of the season were to be informed only on the Thursday of each week what their matches would be on the following Saturday, thus giving pools promoters no time to circulate their lists. Sunderland immediately protested that there was no time for publicity or arranging railway excursions. Football club supporters in isolated instances decided on a boycott.

February 23 : Wholesale protest and a demand for League Management Committee to reconsider its decisions. Leeds United passed a resolution which was tantamount to a vote of censure on the Management Committee.

February 24 : Still more protests and a hint that the Management Committee would allow the normal fixture-list at the week-end.

February 25 : Certain clubs considered the possibility of seeking an injunction to restrain the Football League from delaying the publication of fixtures. Everton, whose chairman was the late Mr. W. C. Cuff (he later became League president), protested, along with others against the League's action in interfering with the fixtures and "keeping our supporters in ignorance of the common facts of football."

February 26: Invitation to the 44 major League clubs to attend a meeting at Leeds on the following Monday sent out under the names of Leeds United, Manchester City, Stoke City, Sunderland, Blackburn Rovers, and Newcastle United. There was a meeting of four members of the Management Committee in Manchester, but no statement made. Mr. E. Holland Hughes, secretary of the Pools Promoters' Association, said that: "The promoters were quite satisfied that they had found a satisfactory solution calculated to meet all contingencies."

February 27: A definite statement that all the following day's fixtures had been altered—six clubs notified by telegram. A decision by the Management Committee to call a special meeting of all League clubs for Monday, March 9, in Manchester. An announcement by the Pools Promoters Association that they would accept all coupons in envelopes bearing a cancellation stamp to show posting not later than 3 p.m. on the following day (Saturday).

February 28: Rearrangement of fixtures was more drastic than had been expected. First Division and Third South and North games were brought forward from March 14 and Second Division ones from April 11, but by it Wolverhampton Wanderers and Plymouth Argyle were each left without a match.

March 2: Twenty-six clubs at the meeting in Leeds voted in favour of asking the Management Committee to return to normal fixtures on the following Saturday and ten abstained. It was revealed that an offer of £50,000 had been made by a syndicate (rumoured as having no connection with the pools) to the Football League for the sole rights to use the fixtures the following season as a commercial proposition.

March 3: Statement by the League president, Mr. John McKenna: "There is to be another change of fixtures and, as last week, they will not be made known until Friday. Everything will go on as planned by the League Management Committee."

March 4: To prevent leakage, late telephone calls by the League secretary and not telegrams to notify teams travelling long distances. Further protests.

March 6: Revealed that all the First Division fixtures for that day were brought forward from April 4, all the Second Division ones from March 21, all the Third Division South from April 18, the Third Division North remaniing as originally planned.

March 9: The pools " war " at an end. By a vote of 43 to five, the clubs at the meeting in Manchester decided to ignore the pools and to revert to the official fixture list for the rest of the season. The resolution passed on February 20 declaring the pools to be a menace was rescinded. Mr. C. E. Sutcliffe, the fixture maker, said counsel had advised him that the copyright existed in him but he was ready to hand over everything to the League if desired. The fixtures were compiled from a chart that was his own private property. The meeting agreed that the League Management Committee should confer with Mr. Sutcliffe on the purchase of the rights of the chart. Mr. Sutcliffe said offers had been received from various quarters for the copyright of the fixtures.

So the pools had won without really having to make a serious fight themselves—the clubs and public opinion had done it for them. Even a fight against them in Parliament was defeated. Everyone now realised that the pools were here to stay and they enjoyed an even greater popularity. A vast new industry, employing thousands of people (mainly women and girls) was built up out of Soccer without the sport accepting a penny from it.

To-day, Soccer legislators realise that there is nothing to stop pools wagering. It has got too big a grip on the public. What many leaders of the game would like to see in Britain, however, is State-run pools, with the profits, or some of them, being ploughed back into sport—not wholly Soccer—for the physical and moral development of youth.

The wonderful training centres, stadia, and coaching schemes developed out of State-run pools in countries abroad are the envy of our Soccer leaders. They note that, in simpler methods of pools wagering than our own complicated systems, many of these Continental State-run pools are staged on the results of British matches each week—a very great tribute to the rigorously clean manner in which our Soccer is staged.

Sweden, for instance, has five of these centres throughout the country and it is hoped to build more. Everything is properly organized, with dormitories, dining rooms, gymnasia, playing pitches, indoor and outdoor bathing pools, and facilities for every known form of sport from football to yachting and ski-ing. It is a wonderful system.

Greatest difficulty in the realisation of all these dreams is the attitude of religious-minded people in this country. They do not want the state to recognise, or at least organise, betting of any sort. If they could see a place like Boson, on the head of a Swedish fjord, where schoolchildren as much as anyone else can go to receive its benefits, they might regard it as a means for keeping the youth of this country off the streets and thereby reducing crime. All the young people to be seen there are happy and healthy in mind and body. Each one of them is a living testimony of the benefits which can accrue.

It has been said that the hold which the pools have got on the British people has helped to create the huge extra watching interest we see to-day compared with pre-war. A true story is that one of the best-known officials in the game who takes a delight in paying his 1s. 3d. admission fee to the terraces, stood next to a woman on a particular excursion of his. Eventually, noticing that she did not show any particular enthusiasm for either team, he asked her which side she really followed.

"Neither," came the reply. "I am here because I put a shilling a week on the pools and I just came along to see what it was all about!"

Giving evidence to the Royal Commission on Betting, Lotteries, and Gaming in October, 1939, Mr. Arthur Drewry, President of the Football League, and vice-president of the F.A. said that he thought the Football League considered that pools had, if anything, created more interest and had increased the attendances at football matches.

On the important question of whether betting affects the results of matches, the Football Association made this reply in its memorandum to the Royal Commission:—

"THE Association believes that betting has no influence whatsoever upon the result of any matches played under its jurisdiction. Nevertheless, it is mindful of the fact that if betting were to gain a hold on the game, the present position would be seriously undermined.

"Here it is appropriate to distinguish between three types of betting—ready money, fixed odds, and football pools. The potential danger of each may be summarised as follows:—

" **Ready money betting**: This is by far the most dangerous, and in 1914 a Ready Money Football Betting Bill was introduced into Parliament, but the outbreak of war prevented any further progress. The matter was again taken up by the Association in 1920, when the Bill was passed into law. Whereas the Association has no reason to believe that the results of any matches have been affected by this type of betting, it is recognised that it might prove a very real danger to the game should the law ever be relaxed in its favour. Quite apart, however, from the possible effect on individual matches, this type of betting would bring within the environs of football clubs all the appurtenances usually associated with ready money betting.

" **Fixed odds credit betting**: The Act of 1920, as its title suggests, is directed against the business of ready money football betting. Its limited nature leaves untouched all forms of credit betting at fixed odds. This Association has no information as to the extent to which it exists, but is satisfied that it has no influence upon the results of matches. Indirectly, however, this form of betting undoubtedly affects the attitude of certain sections of spectators at matches in which they have a financial interest. It may well result in barracking of players, abuse of the referee or other unsavoury incidents. For these reasons alone, this Association is rigidly opposed to fixed odds betting, and will enforce the full vigour of its rules against any offender within its jurisdicion.

" **The football pools**: Whereas this Association maintains its opposition to all forms of betting on football, there is no reason to believe that football pools can in any way affect the result of any individual or group of games. The interest of the 'punter' is so dissipated over a number of matches that it would be mathematically impossible to 'arrange' results to ensure a correct coupon. Also, as far as incidents are concerned, spectators are not likely to be so vitally interested in any given match as to lead them to barrack players or abuse officials solely because of an interest in a pool."

In its memorandum, the Scottish F.A. stated that it had no reason to believe that there was any substantial amount of direct betting at any match, apart possibly from some friendly wagers which might be entirely disregarded; that they were satisfied that amongst those who play and those who control matches (players, referees, and linesmen) betting on the matches in which they are engaged does not exist.

While the F.A. and the Scottish F.A. are substantially in agreement that the pools do not lead to incidents by spectators the Football Association of Wales does think that perhaps they do. In its memorandum, it stated:

" The Association is satisfied that the pools do not affect the results of any matches, but fears that when a section of spectators who infrequently become abusive and difficult, it is possibly due to the fact that when the home team loses when considered a certainty to win and entered as such on the spectator's coupon, the conduct referred to is due to a feeling of being let down by the home team."

In supplementing the view of the Welsh F.A., Mr. Milwyn Jenkins in his evidence to the commission said:

" We have no definite proof but, particularly where the smaller clubs are concerned, we have very strong grounds indeed to suspect that, where there is trouble among the spectators, it is influenced by the fact that the home team is losing and the home team is on the coupon to win. Without having actual proof we have had facts laid before us which leave us in no doubt about the position. It is something much stronger than patriotism and loyalty to the home team."

Facts given to the Commission by Sir Stanley Rous, secretary of the Football Association, on the manner in which football pools are staged in other countries are most interesting. He said:—

" I speak first of all of Sweden, where it (football pools) was at one time private enterprise; gradually a committee was set up to grant licences and the percentage of money that was sent to it from the pools for distribution, for the provision of facilities, for equipment, playing fields, and the like, was such that private people were soon out of business.

" In countries where we have studied the setting up of a simple form of pool—they are not so complicated as they are in this country because the promoters there just take twelve matches, nearly all English football matches, on which the pools are conducted— it is not long before the general public and the citizens of those countries see the benefit of them. In Switzerland there are Government representatives on the committee and gets sometimes 70 per cent of the grant which they claim and they soon see players' centres set up from which the youth of the country reaps an advantage. Holland is now considering it. In Northern Germany the amount of money available at the end of one month was £150,000, so it is clear that Germany will soon rehabilitate its sports facilities from these pools. There is a committee there set up to issue licences to the committees who have organized it."

Sir Stanley went on to point out that prizes were very much smaller, but more evenly spread—Continental people prefered it that way.

Professor John Jewkes, a member of the commission, posed these questions: " Does the Football Association think that if a surplus (from football pools in Britain) were available and were used for these various purposes mentioned, that it really is a very good way of providing funds for playing fields and the like? To have to depend on a form of betting which might change in volume at any time? It is a new thing; it came quickly, it might go quickly?"

Mr. Drewry replied: " There is the probability that controls might change, but voluntary subscriptions and other sources of income are often not sufficient to provide grounds, facilities and equipment and many people are thereby prohibited from enjoying any form of recreative physical exercise; under a scheme of this sort they could be provided not only in large areas where the population is great, and where subscriptions can more easily be collected, but also in those localities—I say this because it came to my notice in Norway—where the population is sparse, but where it is very important that the widely separated parts should have some recreative facilities. The Norwegians have blasted flat places out of rocks so that they can set up playing fields. They tell me it would have been quite impossible by any other means. So that it is not only in the generally accepted places that assistance is needed, but in those places where otherwise it would be much more difficult to provide these facilities."

Sir Stanley Rous: " The number of people who used to be able to give not only service but money is diminishing. I think when we go abroad we are a little envious of the magnificent facilities provided as a result of the pools organized on the Football League matches of this country."

That is the brief case-book of football pools. Which is right and which is wrong? Are they best left as they are or run under statutory control? Whether it is one or the other, there is at least the certainty that unless some newer form of wagering is evolved, the pools are here to stay, as football itself admits.

WHAT NEXT IN SOCCER

New communities will call
for a re-shaped League.

NO ONE in Soccer—the legislator, the director, the manager, the player, the spectator, and least of all the pressman—is ever satisfied. And so it should be. The perfect state is always several jumps ahead.

The game has its visionaries and—though it may often be doubted—none more so than at the top. Soccer has never been more popular than it is to-day, even though there are constant reminders that it is not so good as it used to be (which is just a matter of opinion). More countries are playing it, and still more want to raise their present standards not only to that of the British, but past it. Indeed, in certain instances, Britain is being led.

In view of the challenge to our supremacy, therefore, it is perhaps important first of all to examine our position in World Soccer to-day. The manner in which the game was first organized some seventy or eighty years ago in Britain has already been traced, together with subsequent history. Now, wider influences are at work.

Almost the whole world—but not quite, as Neil Franklin has proved—is organized under the F.I.F.A., which has increased its stature considerably since the last war because of the return of the four British Associations.

It is not intended to go into the reasons for the British breakaway, years before, but only to say that F.I.F.A. struggled on, and though making some sort of progress was naturally restricted without our great experience and influence. So, at the end of the last war, " feelers " were put out for the British to resume membership.

We had seriously to consider whether we should try to maintain our lead from where we were, or do it inside some concentrated authority like F.I.F.A. What we could not ignore was the manner in which the whole World was leaping into the game. The British Associations decided to return to F.I.F.A., but it had to be a diplomatic return. It was handled well on both sides.

Important now in a situation which is almost as complicated as U.N.O. is the preservation of tact and sportsmanship. Some up-and-coming countries eventually may dislike and rebel against the strong grip we hold on the game; we on our part may have to concede some important points as our ability and authority are threatened. The greatest factor which will help us to maintain our present position may not be in the council chamber, but on the playing pitch. If our players can keep ahead of all others in sportsmanship and achievement, then will they provide the one clear reason why British Soccer will continue to lead the World.

In England, the two major problems are the question of wages, a subject which has been comprehensively dealt with elsewhere, and the possibility of a further extension of the League system. The Third Division has already been extended by another four clubs, two in each section, but is it enough?

For the moment it is opportune to look back to the end of the first world war, which had given an impetus to new communities. So first the Third Division South was formed in 1920, and the Third Division North the year after. The League spread itself, and though various clubs have had ups and downs, the whole extension has been firmly established. No one would think of removing the Third Division now.

After the second World War, still newer communities opened up, and will continue to do so under the

Is floodlight football one of the next big things in British soccer? There have been various experiments with it. Here is a "shot" from a match between South Liverpool and the Nigerian footballers, most of whom played without boots, and some of them in bare feet.

Photo: Sporting Chronicle.

One of the first of the great — the late Lord
Kinnaird as he was in his playing days. He
figured in nine Cup Finals, was five times on
the winning side, and after his playing days
were over, became President of the F.A.

Reproduction by kind permission

Town and Country Planning Act, which visualises that these fresh centres will be self-supporting both in housing, industry, and amenities, which will, of course, include Soccer. But the game itself is slower in extending itself at home than after the first war. Shrewsbury Town, Scunthorpe United, and Colchester United are now staging League football for the first time in their existence; Gillingham Town were in the Third Division before, but lost their place to Ipswich Town.

Crux of the whole situation is that the power lies in the hands of the First and Second Division clubs, each of whom has a vote, with just four votes (two to each section) going to the Third Division. Naturally taking the view that they must protect their own interests, those First and Second Division clubs have it within their grip to stay as they are, or extend. What would you do if you managed a thriving concern?

What the big clubs fear is that some of their own power will be dispersed—that with more clubs in the League they will find greater difficulty in getting good players, and so on. There are some very effective replies. The huge crowds at Soccer matches since the war have put many grounds out of date; it is impossible to stop populations from growing; the Government is compelled to go ahead and open new communities and Soccer must keep pace with that idea; with proper spotting and coaching schemes, no club ought to be short of players—practically every kid in the country kicks a ball.

Ever since the Football League was first formed it has been compelled by force of circumstance to spread itself—latest extension from eighty-eight to ninety-two clubs is further admission of that. Where will it end—with every professional club in the country

F

under the jurisdiction of the League? There will be great opposition to that, but is it not the ultimate?

The greatest incentive in League football is promotion and relegation, and there are cogent arguments in favour of it being afforded to many more clubs. Champions of the Southern League, the Midland League, the Cheshire County League, the North-Eastern League, and so on, get no more than the satisfaction of finishing on top. No promotion and no relegation. The same old round each season. But what an incentive the whole game would get if opportunity were given for a club to go on mounting the scale on its own merit!

Portsmouth provide the most recent first-class example. One of the original members of the Third Division in 1920, they have won the Cup, and now the League championship in successive seasons.

Then there is the case of a club in Sweden, where the whole country is organized in one League. That club came from a village where there were only 800 inhabitants, won its way to the Swedish First Division, but is now back in the Fourth. In other words, it has found its own level, but the opportunity was there for it to take. There will always be successes and failures. Even if the League were extended to embrace every professional club in the country there would be many who could not avail themselves of the chance to rise. But conversely, there would be many who would.

The number of non-League clubs who are capable of paying the present Football League wage scale is remarkable. Their problem, of course, might be increased if players eventually force their claims for private agreements, but even Arsenal could not pay too many men fabulous salaries. It is reasonable to expect, therefore, that such a situation would solve itself, as most problems do in time.

Since the last war, there have been three ideas for an extension greater than that recently passed. They are :—

(1) Formation of a national Third Division with two Fourth Divisions (North and South).

(2) Retention of the Third Division in its old form (twenty-two clubs in each section), with two Fourth Divisions (North and South) added, and

(3) Retention of the Third Division, with a new competition called the Intermediate League, with promotion to and from the Third Division.

The Intermediate League is the latest idea, but there are some doubts whether forty-four new clubs could be found strong enough to form it in North and South sections—sixteen clubs in each, following the pattern of the Scottish " A " and " B " Divisions is most favoured.

Best scheme of all, however, is the first. At the end of any given season, the eleven clubs finishing at the top of each section would the next season form one national Third Division of twenty-two clubs. That would leave twenty-six to form the nucleus of a Fourth Division, into which the eighteen best non-League clubs could be voted to form two sections. It would strengthen the structure of the League; the two other schemes are apt to leave it straggling.

Beyond the Fourth Division or the Intermediate League, there has been no serious thought; these ideas for the moment have been considered enterprising enough. But is there any valid reason why the country should not be broken down still more under the jurisdiction of the League into North-West, South-West, North-East, and South-East Leagues with promotion and relegation to and from a Fourth Division? Or is that thinking too far ahead?

There are those within the administration who see the tremendous possibilities of such a reorganization, and although the processes are slow, they may one day see them come true. The incentives are great.

Another suggestion which comes more from the direction of the Football Association is to cut down the number of clubs in each division of the League from twenty-two to eighteen thereby restricting the League programme to thirty-six matches a season for each club instead of the present forty-four.[42] It is considered that the public becomes wearied of a long League struggle, and that in making it more compact, provision would be made for more Internationals, Inter-League, Inter-City, and Inter-Town games, in which clubs from the same centres would join to put out teams against joint sides from other places.

This, of course, might open the way to the formation of a British League, about which there has been talk from time to time. For instance, we may see the great sides from Glasgow combining forces to meet those from London, Birmingham, and elsewhere. The idea has much to commend it, although naturally the clubs are not willing to have their own League programme curtailed unless there are suitable safeguards against loss.

What next? Floodlight football? That's not new. Why, Blackburn Rovers played two matches under electric light in 1878. First one was against Darwen, but as they could scarcely see the ball, they had it painted white when they played a similar match against Accrington just afterwards. They had one lamp at each end of the ground, the game started at seven o'clock in the evening, 6,000 people paid for admission, and there were thousands more getting a free peep from the hillsides.

They play floodlight football in North and South America—and the alternative of daylight or floodlight was offered in the World Cup at Rio to those countries who wanted it. Various attempts have been made to stage Soccer matches in this country under artificial light, one of the latest being at South Liverpool for the visit of the barefooted Nigerians.

Liverpool liked it when they played in America and Canada and say that the grass looks greener than in daylight! They are watching developments, and so are a few more clubs. The difficulties of shade and dazzle are now overcome. The right reaction from the public would almost surely lead to a new mid-week competition at nights.

When the time comes for clubs to get the building licences necessary to reorganize their grounds, flood-lighting may be installed as a necessary asset. And some of our grounds do need reorganizing. The splendid national stadium at Lisbon, and the new stadium they built at Rio for the World Cup finals are two direct pointers, quite apart from others. Of course, foreign countries who started playing football long after us have an advantage in ground planning. While some of the things they have done may be impossible in many of our centres, there is no reason why a few of them might not be embraced in any future ground planning or improvements.

Why should a football ground be used virtually only once a week for eight months of the year? Why shouldn't social clubs be formed—places to which supporters could go during the week, and where youngsters could receive training? It would all make for increased interest in a club—and the young footballer properly coached from an early age would be a fine asset. It would ensure a first-class flow of recruits into the game and make for even bigger crowds.

With sufficient gymnasia attached to football grounds it would be possible to stage five-a-side indoor leagues and cup competitions, both senior and junior, indoor tennis tournaments, gymnastic displays, and the like. The public would love it—and it would all bring in extra revenue.

It is imperative, too, with the challenge which is coming from the new element, television, which seems to be the only solution to all those disappointed millions who cannot get a ticket to see the Cup Final. There never will be a ground big enough to hold that spectacle, nor, possibly, those England-Scotland Internationals.

There is something to be said for being able to snuggle down in an armchair by the fireside on a bad day to watch a sporting spectacle, and especially a football match, but without the cash customer there would be no big spectacle.

The Association for the Protection of Copyright in Sport has been formed to safeguard the interests of sports promoters, which also means football club managements. Altogether, something like seventy or eighty sports, including the major ones, banded together to fight not domestic television, but its re-diffusion to cinemas and other public places on sporting occasions.

The major sports naturally dislike the idea of someone else getting the rake-off for something they have spared neither effort nor expense to put on. They want a share of any re-diffusion profits to cover what they might lose by allowing television. In other words, there is a fight over your patronage, dear public. That's why it is imperative that football grounds be brought up to date for the better comfort of everyone as quickly as possible.

Sunday football? Here's a problem. Thousands upon thousands of youngsters are playing it not only because they like it but because there are not enough grounds available on Saturday afternoons. So far, the Football Association has refused to legislate for it but a separate body, the Sunday Football Association, has been formed, declaring its independence and trying to give to the Sunday footballer just the same status as those who play on Saturdays and other days of the week.

There have been hints of forming a national Sunday Football League, with various divisions and promotion and relegation. Once that is done, it is believed public support would eventually be bigger than on Saturdays.

There are snags, however. Big snags. Suitable grounds are the main problem. The Football League clubs are naturally not going to lease their enclosures for Sunday play. Even non-League clubs, affiliated to the F.A. like their bigger brethren, are too fearful of incurring the displeasure of higher authority. Moreover, the Lord's Day Observance Act, which gives opportunity to the informer, is another powerful deterrent.

The F.A. is watching the situation closely, remembering that the Continental Sunday is coming more and more to the people but respectful of the still powerful opinion of strict Sabbatarians. It is a peculiar position for them, because this tremendous Sunday soccer overflow is a direct result of the F.A.'s own efforts to popularise the game. The Sunday footballer of to-day is a vastly different fellow from those who played for pints. Many of them even go to Sunday school or Church before or after their game!

Soccer demands a constant watch on the future. Even the composition of teams may be altered to make for more open, faster play. Or is that asking too much? The imagination can run riot in trying to foresee what will come next. Maybe it is advisable just to let these few ideas sink in.

PART TWO

Great
Names

by

ARCHIE LEDBROOKE

WERE THESE THE BEST?

A Cavalcade of Soccer's immortals
from Kinnaird to Wright.

SINCE football became an organised game in place
of an impromptu recreation, thousands of soccer
players have passed into and out of the sporting
firmament. Here and there have been the brighter
ones, the stars of the game, and there the simile must
be halted. Science can measure heavenly stars and
state accurately the degrees of brightness, the size,
even name the chemicals; in sport, ability is largely a
matter of opinion. Box-office appeal is even more
dependent on personal tastes. No one, no matter how
skilful he may be in his appraisement of the playing
qualities and necessities, no matter how free he may
be of prejudice, no matter how fresh his recollections
of an age that is gone, can declare with emphasis
" Meredith was better than Matthews ", or strike a
wager that " Bloomer was better than Mortensen ".
He may express his views forcibly, give cogent
reasons, carry the argument to its limit . . . but it's
all just a matter of opinion.

One of the difficulties of making comparisons between players of various ages of the game is that one
is hardly ever free of some kind of prejudice. The
veteran reporter, it is found, is all too easily led to
praise the old at the expense of the new; the boy who
has paid his pence to stand in the rain out on the
slopes of Stamford Bridge or Maine Road simply cannot credit that there was ever a better inside forward
than Tommy Walker or a finer full-back than Bert
Sproston.

The fact is that the word " better " should not be
used at all. In the international class players are

different from each other, not better or worse.

Fashions change. Crowds come to expect different methods. The very line-up of the teams was altered when the off-side law was varied, so that the centre-half, the glorious giant who could roam the field and impose his will on the pattern of play, became instead the most anonymous man on the field—the stopper. So how could Leslie Compton be worse or better than Alec Raisbeck?

Have you ever seen Parola, the Italian centre-half, playing for his country? Dark-skinned, long-legged, he affects very short pants. His shirt is a flimsy nothingness. Not a perfect player, but a jolly good one. Now look at Geoffrey Green's picture of the Hon. A. F. Kinnaird, that historic figure who played in nine Cup Finals and was on the winning side in five of them: " . . . he took the field ready for battle, for a battle it was in those days with the shoulder charge freely given and taken, and some friendly hacking thrown in for good measure, in spite of the rules. Kinnaird, a half-back, wore long white flannel trousers, his jersey, and a blue and white quartered cricket cap. And to round it off, he was the proud owner of a splendid red beard."

How can you compare the two? You cannot: you can only read, and marvel at the outstanding ability of them both. Parola, with his knack of letting his legs fly, looks the picture of athletic grace; how, you may wonder, could Kinnaird move quickly, turn economically — why, the famous drawing makes him look more like a man about to take the rope in a tug-o'-war. Yet we are told that Kinnaird dribbled clean through the rival team to score one dramatic Cup Final goal, and when Old Etonians beat Blackburn Rovers at The Oval in 1882, he did not merely jump for joy; he stood on his head in front of the pavilion. Could Parola do **that?**

One of the first great players whose name is still remembered was R. W. S. Vidal, of the Wanderers, known to all footballers as " the prince of dribblers ". (Can this be the man so scornfully dealt with by Sir Osbert Sitwell for his lack of ability in teaching a small and sensitive boy so soon to grow to genius?).

Vidal could, and did, dribble half the length of the field without being dispossessed. Yet did not an Irishman perform something like this when Sammy Smyth of Wolverhampton Wanderers spanned fifty or sixty yards of Wembley turf before shooting past the Leicester City goalkeeper?

Beauty, in football, may or may not lie in the eye of the beholder. The professional manager may prefer the severely practical player to the artist, and is apt to give the offender a taste of his tongue if he catches a man trying to beat more than one opponent. So for the club manager we record the arrival of the first really combined team, the Old Carthusians of 1881, but at this period everything was soon to be dominated by the arrival of professionalism, at first a trifle of smuggling an odd player in, then so widespread that it was legalised in the mid-eighties. And then came the Football League, with it a new era in soccer, and the Preston North End Invincibles who won the Cup and League in 1888-89: Mills-Roberts; Howarth, Holmes; Drummond, Russell, Graham; Gordon, James Ross, John Goodall, F. Dewhurst, and Thompson. To this day the name of Goodall is respected, one of the first of the great professionals.

When Preston North End were in special training for one of their Cup Finals of the '30's, Goodall turned up to see them. A tallish, big-boned man, but not very big in sum, he was very quiet, talked sense when he did speak, and had nothing but good to say of the modern professional. One pictures him as a severely utilitarian player, discarding frills, an assumption based on the personal character of the man that is justified by the records of the game.

Goodall not only helped to cradle football, but he lived long enough and played long enough to see developments which would have staggered the old officials of North End, a club which played rugby in the early eighties. He moved to Derby County, played alongside Steve Bloomer, did not give up football until he was 50, and at the end actually sampled Southern League football, where ambitions and aspirations were already pointing the way to a wide expansion of first-class football.

It is so difficult to arrive at a true estimate of the worth of the men of those times—it's all like trying to conjure up a picture of W. G. Grace batting to Arthur Mailey and Aubrey Faulkner. But the writer met a man in Stresa, one lovely spring day, who had no doubts about the skill of Preston North End. The English team were training there for their match—and one of their greatest victories—against Italy, and this veteran was staying in the same hotel. And he swore that about the year 1888, or it may have been a little later, he saw Preston North End play Bolton Wanderers. The Bolton men were worthy opposition and with North End taking things a little on the easy side, Bolton scored first. The ball was middled for the re-start, and the North End inside forwards, nettled by the goal, proceeded to show what they could do. They dribbled and inter-passed the ball up to the Bolton goalkeeper, took it past him into the net, and then dribbled and passed it back to the middle again.

This cannot be a catalogue of all the fine players of all the fine teams. We must slip along through the ' 80's and '90's when the Midlands and the North were striving for supremacy, when Sheffield and Nottingham matched the Birmingham area, and Lancashire held its head high.

The names linger on the tongue as they recall the great games of great days.

Nick Ross of Preston North End, who from all accounts must have been one of the finest of all full-backs; the Walters brothers; N. C. Bailey; Wreford Brown, a great player who became an equally great legislator; E. C. Bambridge; Allen of the Wolves, an outstanding centre-half; W. N. Cobbold, and the rest.

There was the beautiful Villa side of 1896-7, which won both Cup and League with such men as Howard Spencer, Athersmith, Devey, and the half-back line of Reynolds, Cowan, and Crabtree. Cowan was the captain and centre-half perfect, although the Villa wondered for a brief spell when they had to suspend him for obtaining leave by a little piece of deception so that he could secretly train for the Powderhall Handicap (which he duly won along with a packet of money).

Cowan was the hub of the sequence of Villa half-back lines which set up a tradition; be strong at half-back, and you need not worry. The method persisted until the mid-twenties, and then the accent shifted to inside forwards. But that thought takes us from footballers to football, and here it is with individuals we are mostly concerned. We are still in the '90's, and it has to be recorded that Billy Bassett appeared on the scene, a little winger of infinite grace just as, in old age, when he was chairman of West Bromwich Albion he had a courtesy all his own and a sober approach to football's problems. He was incapable of a harsh word, and it is easy to imagine that he was equally incapable of a football move that was not perfectly poised. Easy to imagine that his moves were bird-like in their lightness, tigerish in their winning effectiveness.

The Gibson and Pickford history says of Bassett: " He was not a giant in stature, but he was a giant at the game. He brought to bear upon it every grain of intellect and brain power which he possessed, and a generation hence old stagers will be speaking of him as the greatest big-match player of their time. . . . In an international Bassett was the safest card that England had in her hand."

And the authors recall a famous cup-tie when the Albion beat Notts Forest at Derby in a blinding snowstorm. The whirling flakes did not upset Bassett who repeatedly sprinted half the length of the field and put over the centres for each of Albion's six goals.

There was Hugh Wilson in the fine Sunderland side, a half-back with a giant's vigour and who spent it prodigally. Sunderland, a jewel in football's firmament, had no brighter gem than Wilson who, it was said, could single-handed hold up a whole attack. There were great half-back lines in this era of soccer, now going through a Golden Age in company with cricket, and at Sheffield United there was Nudger Needham, generally rated the most natural footballer of them all, a man who never required teaching but who did the right thing by instinct. It was many years before such another appeared on the field, and then an English international selector said that Billy Wright was the nearest approach to Needham by reason of the easy way he slipped into first-class football and his all-round skill.

And then arrived, only slightly younger than Bassett, the great G. O. Smith, a centre-forward—and the really first-class centre-forwards are as scarce as fast bowlers, and always have been. All accounts of his play show him up as the complete footballer. He was a deadly shot, yet excelled at passing. His frail build was no handicap, because he used his brains, had skill in his boots and " fought his way to the front by sheer diplomacy ". A Corinthian, he dropped easily as by Divine Right into the full international side alongside the leading professionals of his day.

Into the twentieth century: along with R. S. McColl, who burst into the Scotland v. England matches, the greatest game of the year at this period of football, with the effect of a shell exploding, and the peerless Alec Raisbeck, who came along just after James Cowan. And then Bobby Templeton, one of the half-dozen wingers of whom the connoisseurs speak with piety. A temperamental, dancing-master footballer, unusually reliant on sympathetic partners for one so clever, a man of moods—yet invariably finding the right mood for the big occasion.

As the new century moved along, so came Vivian Woodward of whom it was said " He made things so easy for the people around him to play football". Whereas G. O. Smith, an amateur, adopted generally the methods of the professionals with whom he played for his country, Woodward retained an individualistic style; he always **looked** an amateur. He was never mechanical, had no set tactics, relied on his football brain to solve in an instant each problem as it arose, and was able to hold his own in the best company long enough to win a record total of caps.

Steve Bloomer has a place all his own in English football history. It is said of him that in late middle age he was standing on the Derby County ground with a broom in his hand, somewhere near the edge of the penalty area, while some of the players were kicking the ball about.. A couple were talking to the old international. The ball suddenly came across waist-high, and the two younger men ducked. Next thing they knew was that the old international had dropped the broom and the ball was in the back of the net. It may be true or not; the story however has this point—Bloomer's football theme was that the game was won by goals scored. He could, and did, shine at the other branches of soccer, but it was as a marksman that he stood supreme. As soon as he could see the white of the penalty line, he said, he thought about shooting.

James Catton called him the pale-faced warrior of football, and a man who played with and against him has related how he could tackle and how he swerved his passes to make interception difficult. He must have been a very completely-equipped player, and although so slightly built he was absolutely fearless in facing the rough type of back in which the game then abounded. If the ball was not in his vicinity, it was written, he looked on in languid interest. We shall make a comparison and a contrast later on with his modern counterpart.

Through many years there was the full-back partnership of Crompton and Pennington, the Blackburn Rovers man with his stooping tackle and his kick up the side-line which was re-born with John Carey after the second world war, and Pennington, an upstanding man who, they say, cried on the field when Barnsley scored the winning goal in the Cup Final re-play of 1912.

Jocky Simpson, English-born but so long denied an international cap, returned to this country and joined Blackburn Rovers, gained his rightful place in the 'national team, and left behind him the reputation of being able to centre from any position at any angle.

All this time forwards gained individual esteem, but the half-back line was the basis of every team's worth Yet we must not forget the one man who can lose a game in a fraction of a second: the goalkeeper. H. J. Arthur of Blackburn Rovers began a long line of outstanding English internationals in this position, and there were J. W. Sutcliffe, W. R. Moon, and J. W. Robinson, the last-named possibly unsurpassed in all-round excellence in the last line of defence.

We shall come back to goalkeepers, but must break off to mention a Welshman whose name is as much

a part of football's story as Rhodes's is of cricket:
Billy Meredith, the winger who came from Chirk,
played for both Manchester City and Manchester
United, and became the standard by which all wingers
are judged. He was fast, he had superb balance, he
was always fit, he practised incessantly, he had the
most accurate back-heel the game has known, he
scored a total of goals which is variously put by experts at from two hundred to four hundred, he played
until he was forty-nine years of age, he could centre
to drop the ball on a man's head, he had a pair of
bandy legs which were the delight of cartoonists.
Like Wilfred Rhodes, he became a legend in his own
life-time.

And about this time there were two centre-half
backs striving for supremacy—Wedlock and Roberts.
They say that Wedlock was generally preferred by
the international selectors because Roberts, like so
many of the Manchester United men, was a Players'
Union man through and through.

Once Wedlock had edged Roberts out of the English team, the Manchester man could not get back,
and the controversy as to which of the pair was the
more effective player was the football topic of the day.
Wedlock held on to his place and his caps, but Roberts
enjoyed one triumph over his rival. The gods fash-
ioned things so that Manchester United met Bristol
City in the Cup Final of 1909, and it was Roberts who
finished on the winning side. He was a biggish man,
broad in the shoulder, a bundle of energy who employed a slashing pass out to the wings and who
drove his forwards on as though he stood behind
them with a whip. Wedlock was short, neat and
light on his feet in spite of his weight, and apparently
made of rubber.

Dashing Harry Hampton arrived, the greatest
possible contrast to Smith and Woodward. He had

one idea in life: to propel himself and ball towards the other end of the field in the shortest space of time, and then to smash the ball between the posts. He revitalised a clever but shot-shy Aston Villa team, led the forward line to two Cup Final triumphs, and after finding fame in a few weeks after his arrival at Villa Park, held it for years. His unrestrained style brought back to football, given too closely to short passing, the swinging kick from centre to wing, and wing to centre, which had marked the play of West Bromwich Albion in their palmy days.

The Newcastle United side came to its peak and its Cup disappointments. McCracken, the crafty back whose name is forever associated with the off-side trap and the subsequent change in the law which altered the fact of the game; Veitch, a man who talked and wrote football as well as he played it; McWilliam, to find later fame as manager of Tottenham Hotspur's most successful team; Albert Shepherd, a centre-forward of driving energy; some missed a winner's medal, but McCracken and Veitch were there when at long last the Cup was won in 1911.

Bert Freeman just had time to impress his name on football when the first world war broke the pattern of the Cup and the League. Football had arrived as the sport of the million, and when the game was resumed it leapt to a new popularity. There was Grimsdell, a half-back who scored goals. Billy Walker and Clem Stephenson in the Villa team. Charles Buchan (from the pre-war Sunderland side), a tall, thin man of rare ball-playing skill, and whom the selectors said was too clever for the men around him. Sam Hardy, most esteemed of all modern goalkeepers. Frank Barson, an iron man of sport. Andy Ducat, a double international like Harry Makepeace. The flashing Dimmock, whose short career was long enough to make a mark. McCall of Preston North

End, a centre-half fit to rank with Roberts. And then the dawn of the sensational Huddersfield Town team of whom it is hard to choose one man. There was W. H. Smith, the winger who seemed to glide past opponents. Alec Jackson, all flamboyance and action. Goodall at full-back. And working quietly like a mole, Clem Stephenson, who once said of the great sports writer James Catton; " He was always in the know. He used to forecast the English team, and always got ten right. I was the one he got wrong." Strange indeed are the ways of selectors; Buchan played in only four full international matches, Stephenson in but one.

Football was " bigger ". More first-class clubs, more players, more space in the newspapers. Reputations were made more easily, so we must be careful how we name the men lest we place the mediocrities in this select company.

Bob Kelly: no one will quibble at his inclusion, at any rate. A player of poetic rhythm, of style, who seemed unrelated to the hurly-burly of a first-class football match yet survived it all, a quiet spoken little man who came from a part of Lancashire where they think more of an oval ball, and who drifted out of the game as quietly as he played.

Then those two goal-scoring inside forwards Joe Smith and David Jack, together at Bolton, later parted when Jack went to Arsenal, first of the ten thousand pound footballers as Alf Common had been the first of the one-thousand men. Jack, nervous as a race-horse, but always master of his nerves, tall and angular, with a fluttering foot; Smith, built like a bullet and just as damaging. On Smith's left hand was Ted Vizard, another of the quiet kind, who sprang to fame in one season and went to his Welsh home for a civic reception when he was barely old enough to shave. The names crowd on, and then the change in the off-side law brought a new focus on inside for-wards. They became the key-men in place of the old centre-half backs; the pivot became a third back and a strong kicker, a stopper.

About this time there was Harry Hibbs in goal for England, a fit custodian to follow such as Arthur Robinson, the gigantic Foulke, Sam Hardy, Dick Pym, and J. W. Sutcliffe. Hibbs, like Hardy, mastered the knack of positional play so that he often seemed to be waiting for the shot. Then came Woodley, and after him the boyish Frank Swift, big but agile, who was the opposite of everything that Hibbs stood for in football yet just as effective. Last-second dives, sprawling grabs, risky feats of athletic skill, and all done with a broad smile and a huge enjoyment. Bert Williams of the Wolves is somewhere between the two, a pretty goalkeeper whose back bends like an archer's bow when he soars to reach a ball near the bar.

Just before another war disturbed the pattern of the game, there were such men as Ted Drake, a centre forward of size and speed and shooting power. A full-back in Eddie Hapgood who employed bold methods in going up-field to pin his winger and who bore comparison with Cresswell, Cooper, Wadsworth. There was Eric Brook, the volatile winger of Man-chester City, and an energetic half-back Wilfred Cop-ping of Leeds United and Arsenal. England would have been in a bad way without this pair when we played Italy at Highbury in 1934.

Alex James, with his baggy pants, his witty method of playing, in the Arsenal forward line which also included Jack, the flying Hulme, and the boy wonder Bastin, made himself one of the immortals, and people talked of James alongside the old Bobby Walker and Napoleon McMenemy and Patsy Gallacher.

Away in the north-east a new star arose; Horatio

Carter. A little man, seemingly fragile until you noticed the thickness of the knees, and the fire with which he broke through a tackle. There was an Irishman, too, Peter Doherty, who went from Blackpool to Manchester City and then to Derby County and on to Huddersfield Town and then to Doncaster Rovers, perhaps never bettered as an effective inside forward. With his flapping legs, his curious twists and turns and feints, he ran and ran and ran. He would run himself to a standstill in two or three years, they used to say of him, but his opponents tired first. He made goals for other people, yet in Manchester City's championship season he helped himself to thirty of the best.

As Carter and Doherty came in, Hugh Gallagher was enjoying his last great days. A square little man, saucy with the ball, saucy with his repartee, there seemed nothing beyond his prowess. There is a special place in the gallery of football's immortals for Gallagher, who showed that the legends of the old dribblers could be true by doing the same things himself.

We have not many " home " Scotsmen in this gallery of ours, which is concerned chiefly with the men who have built the structure of English football, but a place must be found for Alan Morton, the Wee Blue Devil who confused and confounded his rivals for so many years until there was hardly a back to be found in England capable of taking him on. There was Bob McPhail, an inside forward of strength and skill in a happy combination, perhaps the ideal type to suit a professional manager. And Cunningham and Meiklejohn, too.

Now comes Stanley Matthews, an enigmatic winger able to kill a ball stone dead whether it reached him fast or slow; who can head a ball beautifully but hates doing it; who can baffle a man by wriggling his hips; who has speed so that no back in the four countries can live with him. A man who finds it hard to talk about football, but is not necessarily without ideas on soccer. Scrupulously clean, his look of reproach directed towards a tough opponent can be read by the whole crowd. They called him The Wizard at Stoke, and then he went to Blackpool with whom he played a Cup Final only to join the long list of great players never to take home a winner's medal. He fills grounds wherever he plays, he causes controversy not of his own seeking and is liked most by those who know him best.

In haste to cover the ground, we have passed by William Ralph Dean and must pause to consider him. A tallish, dark, man he broke and still holds the Football League scoring record. They say of him now that he was the finest header of a ball ever to play (shades of that mysterious figure, Leiutenant Sim of the Royal Engineers, said to be the first habitual header!) and possibly too much emphasis has been placed on this feature of Dean's play. We are apt to forget that he was able to shoot fiercely on the run, that he had a stride which positively ate up the ground, that he made goals for other people just as Smith and Woodward did in their different ways, and that he fitted comfortably into an Everton team which played their own brand of football and which could be recognised as the Everton pattern whether they played in their own blue shirts or any old colour. There was a sequence of movement, an unhurried yet rapid system, which was labelled " Goodison " as surely as Jack Hobbs's push to cover-point was labelled " Oval ".

The crowd loved Dean, and they called him Dixie because of his dark skin and his mop of black hair. He disliked the nickname, but he should accept it as a compliment. It was the greeting of the terraces to a man who was one with them, and who gave them so much pleasure.

A comparison and a contrast with the modern Bloomer was promised. He is Stanley Mortensen, English-born with a name inherited from a Scandinavian grandfather. During the second world war he gathered goals galore, and then came the test of peace-time football with its struggle for points and its closer marking and tackling. Mortensen surmounted the difficulties. His fair skin, his unruffled hair, his neat way of dressing, combine to make him look like a stage star rather than a professional footballer, and he has something of the theatrical in his make-up. His dazzling style of play is known all over Europe and those who have watched him will be interested to read these words **written of Bloomer 45 years ago:**

" When the supreme moment comes, he pounces upon the ball like a greyhound, darts past an opponent, swerves towards open ground, and, almost before flurried backs and astounded goalkeeper know what has happened, the ball is in the net. . . . He is full of wire and whipcord, and usually as hard as nails. . . . He has made himself the power he is and has been by reason of an irrepressible desire to conquer."

Those words are just as true of Mortensen, but there is one difference. Bloomer could stand, one hand on hip, watching the play in another quarter of the field. For Mortensen, to stand idle is agony. He wants to join in the fun, to be pulling his weight all the time, and there is in existence a photograph which tells the Mortensen story: Blackpool were defending in a famous cup-tie against Wolverhampton Wanderers, and the picture shows Mortensen, centre-forward, **crouching behind his own goalkeeper,** ready to die rather than surrender.

Contemporary with him is Neil Franklin who **has**

shown that, in an age of stoppers, it is possible for a centre-half to play football. One of the finest sights in the game is to see Franklin secure the ball from a forward and then bustle round him, working his way clear before making a pass. He rarely uses the long ball, but he makes a short pass to an inside forward or a wing-half in such a way that he always seems to have a split second to spare amid all the confusion of the gmae.

Billy Wright has been mentioned, and so we come to the end of the walk through this portrait gallery. Some famous names have doubtless been omitted, some personal favourites overlooked. It is hopeless to attempt to say that this inside-left is better than that one, or that this full-back made fewer mistakes than the other. And if an eleven is named, it is not on all fours with the old schoolboy pastime of choosing a cricket team to play Mars, but a quick scribbling of eleven names. It is not named as a best-ever eleven, but merely as a team of men who have all played in England, and whom it would be nice to see play together: Robinson; Crompton, Pennington; Willis Edwards, James Cowan, Needham; Jackson, Bloomer, Gallacher, Doherty, Templeton.

The reader can pick a "better" team? That is undisputed, anyone can to his taste. Yesterday or to-morrow one's own selection might be different. That happens to be the team of the moment, suitable to a present whim, the team a genie might call up for us.

THE LAUGHING CAVALIER

Alec Jackson,
Wembley Wizard on the Wing.

ALEC JACKSON was a great footballer. And having said that of him, one has not covered the subject by half. He lives on, and will live, as one of the finest outside rights the game has known, but more than that he was a character. He had that vague something which we call personality. He had everything that goes to make up a first-class entertainer.

It is a sure way of provoking an argument among serious-minded soccer folk to mention Meredith, Matthews, and Jackson in one sentence. You can then light your cigarette, sit back, and let the others do the arguing. Just suggest to half a dozen football people that you are not sure which one of the three you would like to have in your select side to play the men from Mars next time they come on a tour; your pleasure is fixed for the evening, just listening to the others. They won't settle it at the end, of course, because it's like the Grace-Hobbs-Bradman-Trumper tussle in cricket, but you will hear a lot of good football sense talked if the others in the company know their business.

This is not going to be a three-cornered fight over the three names. This piece is all about Jackson, and the first thing to mention is that he is the late Alec Jackson. He joined up in the late war, went overseas, and was killed in a lorry smash somewhere near the banks of the Nile. He died as he played—living dangerously.

In temperament, two-footedness, heading ability, footwork, and sheer cheek he was the complete footballer. It is doubtful if any young man, signing professional forms, has ever embarked on his sporting career with greater natural ability, finer equipment from the lavish hand of Nature. The one thing lacked by Jackson was the appreciation that not even a Jackson can play for year after year without hard training. It all came so easily to him in the beginning that the tiresome business of trotting round the cinder track on Tuesday or undergoing the even more boring business of road-work on Wednesday seemed so unnecessary. For ordinary mortals—he could understand that. But for him? He could snatch a goal on Saturday and forget the other days.

There seemed absolutely no limit to what he could do. There was a cup-tie in which Huddersfield Town met Bury about 1930. They played first on the tidy, compact ground at Gigglane, and made a draw of it. The return at Huddersfield was obviously going to be a bit difficult for Bury, so they made plans which differed from the first; they brought in the recently-injured Tiny Bradshaw at centre-half and moved Norman Bullock to wing-half, with a special mission to play wide and keep Jackson out on the wing. (Bradshaw, a towering centre-half who for a season or so was possibly as good as anything ever seen in the position, had been one of the Wembley Wizards a year or two earlier. Grievously injured, he made a wonderful come-back, and was transferred to Liverpool where he did magnificient work in new colours. This tie at Huddersfield really marked the beginning of his come-back).

The plan worked perfectly for most of the game. Bradshaw stopped up the middle and Bullock, a hard tackler and a practical, rather than a pretty, player, watched Jackson. The outside right, looking at the game as a whole, was mastered by a rival who was clever in the essentials, fast, and able to remember his orders. Bullock beat Jackson on points: but you look up the records, and you find that Huddersfield won the tie—with three goals from Jackson.

How did he score them? Ah, that was Jackson's secret. He stole into the centre when no one dreamed that play was about to swing there. But his instinct was uncannily accurate: the play DID swing there. And once Jackson was in the penalty area with the ball bobbing anywhere near by, then the touchline artist became a raging, tearaway goal-getter, taking a chance of injury if necessary, as goal-hungry as Bradman was run-hungry, a match-winner supreme.

There was another cup-tie, a semi-final at Manchester's Old Trafford, when Sheffield Wednesday and Huddersfield were the rivals for a place at Wembley. The form of both sides was well known, both as to individuals and team tactics. Both sides had ample chance to plan their defences, to map out their own styles of play. Both were very fine teams. It was like a game of chess on an out-sized board, a board as big as a football pitch.

How Sheffield Wednesday lost the tie is to-day something of a mystery, even to those who played in it. The one known fact is that Jackson scored both of Huddersfield's goals. Twice he stole into the middle, and twice he put the ball into the net. One of them, the Wednesday players claimed, was handed in. But Jackson's manoevre was so quick, the fatal thrust delivered with such a lightning gesture, that it baffled eyesight.

So Town went to Wembley, and there they met the Arsenal. About this time a story went the rounds that Jackson stood to win a fortune on this one match. The tale went this way: the player had been talking in a hotel of his team's chances, 'way back in the early days of the season, and a bookmaker had laid him the odds of a thousand to one against Huddersfield Town's winning the Cup and Jackson's scoring in every round. Jackson, it was said, had snapped the bet—five thousand pounds to a fiver.

Was it true? The tale reached the office of a great newspaper, and an experienced reporter was sent to Huddersfield to ask him about it. They met in the darkish passage-way which runs under the stand, and the reporter, accustomed to handling all sorts of people from Prime Ministers downwards (or upwards according to your mood of cynicism) decided on the direct approach. Jackson, as usual, was all smiles. He heard the reporter out courteously and then denied the story. He had to, one supposes. The Football Association would have taken a dim view of a footballer who confessed to betting on his own team and on his own performances. And that was that.

But reactions of the reporter are worth recording. He was, as has been noted, not without experience in handling men and women. Under the stand, in the poor light, he could not see Jackson's expression very clearly. He could catch the smile, and the direct gaze of those curiously "alive" eyes. And to this day he does not know whether Jackson was telling the truth, or not.

The Final followed. And it may be interposed here that, following his denial of the bet, Jackson said "I wish it were true. We shall win the Cup, and I shall score." And he smiled in a fashion which robbed the remark of all conceit.

If that wager was ever struck, it was within twelve inches of being won. Quite early in the game that superb winger W. H. Smith, great in quite a different way from Jackson's greatness, centred the ball over the heads of the massed defenders—the classic centre to the far post. Jackson was there, and unmarked. He flung himself at the ball . . . and headed it, grazingly, on the wrong side of the post.

The Huddersfield inside forwards fell away to

nothingness in the second half, and only W. H. Smith played well. And so Jackson never got his Cup-winner's medal, and we never had the chance to learn if that really was a bet, or just a tale from the tap-room.

Many a man has made a name in Cup-tie football and failed to equal it in other games. Jackson was just as great in a League game played as a routine Saturday-afternoon engagement, just as fine in the testing crucible of an international match. He was one of the Wembley Wizards, that Scottish team of all the talents who beat England 5-1 in 1928 and gave an exhibition which possibly has not been equalled in modern times.

That team lined up: Harkness; Nelson and Law; Gibson, Bradshaw, and McMullan; Jackson, Dunn, Gallacher, James, and Morton.

Every man played well, and the team-work drew praise such as had never previously been written since popular daily newspapers began giving space to sport. Could any one man stand out in such a team on such a day? Impossible? Not a bit of it. Jackson was there with three goals of the five to leave an imperishable stamp on the records.

Early in his football career Jackson went to America and delighted the steel workers with his thrilling method of play. Back to Scotland, and three caps for his country in his first season. Then to Huddersfield, signed by Herbert Chapman, who in him recognised a kindred genius. Invariably at outside-right, Jackson played in 21 cup-ties for the club, and scored nineteen goals. That would have been a good tally for a centre-forward; for a winger it was staggeringly efficient.

To go to Chelsea was a mistake, but London called him, and there he was. The bright lights beckoned as surely as England had beckoned him from Aberdeen. After Chelsea it was almost oblivion, but there was one final flourish yet to come.

Ashton National, an obscure Cheshire club, arranged for Jackson to play for them on a contract of fifteen pounds a week plus a share of the gate receipts over a certain figure. It was a novel scheme, but it failed. A half-fit Jackson, living in London and tired by weekly journeys, could not score the goals which would have pulled in the crowd. After a few weeks the contract was cancelled by mutual consent, and all that was left of Jackson at Ashton was a memory of a man who was sufficient of a sportsman to admit that he had flopped, and who readily gave back a contract which could have crippled the sponsors.

And so we come back to Alec Jackson the man, and his smile.

The reporter who stood in the gloom, trying to unravel Jackson's thoughts as they talked under the stand at Huddersfield, was struck by the smile of the man. That smile! The only word for it is—winning. It won hearts wherever he went, and how many full-backs it disarmed, only Jackson and they knew. With his clean-cut features, his bright eye, the little crinkle of the flesh as the grinned like a schoolboy at first sports-day—here was the wonder-man of football indeed. You simply could not help admiring him on the field, loving him off it.

Not even when decay set in. A picture lingers of him when he was in London, keeping a hotel in the heart of theatreland, growing fat and obviously a little tired of football. The features, once so sharp, were slightly blurred now, the quick, nervous movements were slowed, and the eye more likely to rove as he chatted than in the old days when his concentration was as keen as it was flattering to the listener or talker. Yet still the personality came through; still he had something interesting to say, and now and again the face would light up with that old, magical hint of agelessness, and the visitor was held captive by the spell.

He was the Laughing Cavalier of Football. So long as he could play, he laughed. Jackson's only failing was that he could not treat his play as a profession. When football became work, then Jackson left it. And one has the thought that living was play to him, too, and that by the time he was in his forties there was not much point in living on. And one can only think of him in Elysian Fields, laughing and playing and gifted with eternal youth, and there winning the friendship and love of the immortals.

H

ALEX JAMES AND PETER DOHERTY

Two of the great inside forwards
of the stopper era.

ALEX JAMES was the George Gunn of football. A
jester whose movements were in caricature of others,
yet had something original about them, a funny little
man whose whimsicalities were a licensed feature of
soccer during the time he played.

A shortish man, he first of all gave an impression of
being almost dwarfish, as though he was in perpetual
danger of being overwhelmed by the bigger men
around him. Perhaps he had a knack of shrinking,
or perhaps of just appearing to shrink, because if you
could take your eyes away from his feet for a few
seconds, and examine him closely, you soon realised
that he had pretty broad shoulders and a rubbery,
maleable body designed by Nature to twist and turn,
and . . . and to deceive. Lowering your gaze, you
would appreciate, too, that the legs were stoutly made,
made for football, made to take a lot of hard knocks.
So that was James's first bit of football foolery; he
kidded people (and those people included his rivals)
that he was tinier than he actually was.

If you saw James for the first time—and it is a sad
thing about sport that these wonderful " firsts " cannot be recaptured—you would be struck by his rolling
gait. He moved with the comfortable, ambling
method of a lovable baby bear. But then you saw
that he had complete control of all these movements,
just as Bobby Jones the golfer, with a somewhat
similar rubbery make-up, had absolute control over
the lifts and turns which constituted the perfect golfing action.

But essentially James was a footballer, and so there

are his feet to be considered. And so when you had watched James for a few times, and could cease to be just fascinated, and become analytical, you could see the beautiful design of his play. There could have been hardly anyone who was able, at first sight, to appreciate his football skill. His antics, his unusual approach to soccer, his shuffling feint, the unexpected direction of his passes—all disguised the essential soundness of his methods.

They say that when he left Raith Rovers to join Preston North End, he played for the club in an away match, not having had time to report to Deepdale and settle in, in the usual way. On the way back home one of the players nodded over to James and said to a director of the club: " We're not keeping him, are we?" That story has been told before, and is usually related to show how blind a fellow-professional can be. Surely the comment was a natural one: how could genius drop happily into strange company?

There was never a player who at first glance seemed to indulge in so much frippery, yet there was never a player who actually was so economical of movement, so purposeful in all he did. He never just kicked and hoped.

He would turn, flap his legs inside those baggy pants, feint to back-heel, and it all seemed a circus act. The crowd laughed; this was part of the Saturday afternoon fun. But it wasn't fun to James, it was the serious business, for which he was paid, of sending an opponent running the wrong way. Football to him was a life-work.

Another Preston story is of the invitation to the Deepdale players to attend the opening of a greyhound track. On the day of the event one of the other players asked him was he going?

" Go there?" exclaimed James, " Why should I go

to help advertise a sport which may prove a rival to football?"

That remark summed up the purposefulness of the Scotsman's football.

You have all heard of the famous Arsenal defence, which was designed with a dual purpose—to save goals and to make them. The idea was that if an opposing team attacked often enough and long enough, they would be vulnerable to a quick break-away raid. The other side were, in fact, lured forward to destruction and half the crowd, not understanding, went home muttering " Lucky Arsenal ", sometimes substituting another word for the name of the club.

James was an essential man in this defend-and-breakaway scheme of things, as we shall see in a moment. But first let us consider how he adapted the idea to his own use. There was a game in the North of England when Arsenal, for once in a way, were the persistent aggressors. They attacked, only to find a defence as stubborn as their own, determined to resist all that was thrown at them. The men in red shirts tried the long pass designed to make the defence turn and chase. They tried orthodox short-passing along the line. They tried battering a way down the middle. The thin blue line wavered, became confused, but never broke.

Half-backs played close in, inside forwards drew back, wingers went back to help too. The minutes ticked off towards the final whistle and a goalless draw.

James, standing somewhere in the centre circle, pondered the problem and acted. The ball came to him from a clearance, or it may have been a goal kick, and he killed it. Instead of embarking on the fiftieth attempt to inaugurate a scoring attack, he coolly turned and booted the ball towards his own goal.

He reasoned that if Arsenal could only go back on defence of their own free will, the other side might come forward, and in coming forward might expose themselves fatally. It was a brilliant device, the complete fulfillment of Arsenal's playing tactics. How many professional footballers would have thought of that one?

It does not in the least spoil the story by relating that on this occasion the long pass back was not as accurate as it might have been. The goalkeeper was compelled to chase the ball, and finally to concede a corner. From it a goal was scored. In trying to win the match, James had lost it gloriously.

There is a good deal more to Arsenal's defensive work than many people have given the side credit for, and in the great days of Roberts, Hulme, Jack, Lambert, James, and Bastin, a good deal hinged on James. For if there was one feature of his football above all else, it was his gift of making the long pass, and it was the long ball to the sprinter Hulme which so frequently enabled Arsenal to cover more than half the length of the pitch before the other side could properly position themselves.

Many players essay the long pass to the far wing. It is known as a winning move, and was recognised as such before James came into football. But he perfected its making and though there may have been experts before him, there has certainly been no man since so expertly able to deliver this particular pass.

A ball kicked across the field at a range of forty yards is usually lofted so high that, on arrival somewhere in the vicinity of the winger for whom it is intended, it presents many anxious problems. If it has to be killed first time, it presents a problem of technique. If it is to be allowed to bounce, extra judgement of the " length " of the ball is required, and an opportunity is given to the defence to join in the attempt to collect it. It may be necessary to head it, and that is of no use to a winger whose training, outlook, and chief value are all based on footwork.

James mastered the knack of delivering this long ball with a low trajectory, so that the winger's problems were minimised. If he had done nothing else, that trick would have made him worth his place in most teams. But that was just his outstanding trick; there were many others. How many times he rolled the ball through, at precisely the right speed, for Lambert to chase; how many hours he spent in bringing Bastin from immature boyhood to international manhood; how many plays he worked out with David Jack; how many times he linked with a half-back; how many times he sent the defence running the wrong way without moving the ball—no one has count of these.

Many footballers reach a certain state of development and then play by instinct. James, after a fine career with Preston North End, went to Arsenal, captured by Herbert Chapman and the chance of making money outside football. He improved after making the move, and I do not think Chapman had anything to do with it, only James's own appreciation of the things that matter in football. He discovered that, after a clever piece of fooling with the ball and beating an opponent, the same opponent was able to tackle or worry him from behind. He had got into a habit of stopping or slowing up after beating one man. He therefore improved his game by quickening up after tricking a rival, giving that particular opponent no second chance.

When James is talking to you, his face naturally crinkles, and he sees the funny side of things. He won football matches, and he won hearts, and it is a bit of a shock to see from the record books that he played only eight times for Scotland.

Sometimes he was not released by his club, sometimes he was not chosen, for that is the way of selectors. Probably James saw, and sees, the funny side of that, just as he must have appreciated more than anyone else, the luck of his famous goal in the Cup Final against Huddersfield Town.

Arsenal took a football lesson and a hammering that afternoon at Wembley, but they took away the Cup at the end of it all. There was a free kick away on the left. Memory suggests that it was ten or twelve yards inside the touchline and perhaps just a little short of the penalty area. James stopped to place the ball, Bastin ran on, and the ball was kicked to the winger before Huddersfield Town had assembled themselves or their thoughts.

Here controversy enters the story. Some of the Huddersfield Town players who were near the spot say that James placed the ball, and then kicked it while still holding it—an illegal proceeding, if this be the true version. It was said, too, that the referee had given no signal for play to proceed. But on the other hand there has been emphatic testimony that the referee actually gave a signal, that he was watchful and therefore unlikely to have passed a free kick taken with the ball being held by James's hand.

It all happened very quickly, but not too quickly for the rest of the incident to be etched on the memory. Bastin ran forward after collecting the ball, and then on being challenged by Goodall, passed it back to James, as the little man (there, we have fallen into the trap he laid for so many) ran into the penalty area. Probably he called for the ball, and it may not be mere imagination which jogs the memory into suggesting that he clapped his hands for it. At any rate the boy on the wing did his share by rolling back a lovely pass.

So far the Huddersfield Town defence had been

taken by surprise and was off balance. If James made one more move constructively, the whole point of taking the free kick quickly would have been lost, for the inside forward, the maker of attacks, was in full view of probably eight-elevenths of the Yorkshire side. To carry the surprise move to its logical and successful end, the next kick had to be a shot. Now James was not a crack shot at this stage of his career. So the man who spent most of his time in making chances for other people now had to try to score in the most important match of the year. The mind's eye brings back a picture of a hurried adjustment of balance and step, then a slashing, half-sliced drive.

The ball threaded its way through the players, who seemed motionless. Late in its flight the ball swerved violently, beat the goalkeeper's desperate, sprawling attempt to save the situation, and went into the net.

The Cup was Arsenal's, the second goal being a formality when Huddersfield Town had given up all ideas of defence.

James, one guesses, saw the humour of it all. It was a poor sort of shot, unless you happen to agree with the footballer's axiom that any shot is a good one if it scores a goal; that James himself should score in a Cup Final was, indeed, a grim jest.

Since he retired several players have affected a shambling walk and long pants, but none has ever justified the title " another Alec James ". The advice to young footballers is to study his method, if they can find him or his contemporaries to talk to, and then sort out the fundamentals for their own use. The trimmings they must put on for themselves in keeping with their own characters. It is much easier to be yourself than to be a second James.

One of his best secrets was that he did not do too much with the ball. He was a good player without it because of the constant threat that he might do something by running into position. Exactly the converse was true (and happily is true, because he is still playing football) of Peter Doherty. When he is in form, he cannot have too much of the ball. He wants it all the time, not selfishly, not illogically, but because he likes having it and can do so much that is useful with it.

Peter is an Irishman. He moved from his own country to Blackpool, and then when Sir Lindsay Parkinson died, Blackpool found themsleves temporarily in the position that they could not keep Doherty. Manchester City were one of the clubs interested, and they paid £10,000, a big fee in those days. The officials who negotiated the transfer say that they never had a star who was so easy to sign, and that the talks lasted a very short time as between club and player. Doherty moved to Derby County when the game was about to be resumed after the war, then to Huddersfield Town, and then to Doncaster Rovers as player-manager.

With Manchester City he won a League championship medal; at Derby he won a Cup medal; at Huddersfield he succeeded in helping the club to stay in the First Division when everyone was forecasting immediate relegation and football eclipse; and when he went to Doncaster the Rovers moved from the Third to the Second Division in his first season. There is a record of successes which bespeaks the practical footballer and if James made the crowd laugh, it is true to say that Doherty made them gasp.

Many years ago football people said airily that he would run himself silly. During the war, talking to some other P.T. friends, he himself remarked: " Of course, our time is done." But still he is with us.

Manchester people have seen some pretty good inside forwards with City and United, but no one had ever seen a man run so far as Doherty ran during the season 1936-37 when City won the championship with some of the most brilliant attacking football of our time. On his left was Brook, a bludgeoning winger who scored twenty goals in the season. On his right was Tilson, the Artful Dodger of football, who took fifteen goals. Inside right was usually Alec Herd, with a tremendous shot at long range or from a dead ball. He managed fifteen, too. On the right wing was a dancing master, Toseland, who did not score often, reckoning his task done if he out-sprinted everyone and tossed over to his centres. In the half-back line was Jackie Bray, many times an international, and at full back was Sammy Barkas, good enough to rival Hapgood in the English team. And in goal was Frank Swift, all personality and daring skill. Difficult to shine in such company . . . unless you were a Doherty, making goals for others but scoring thirty yourself in forty-one games! His inside forward play that season touched the heights. It seemed impossible that his frame could stand up to the punishment he inflicted on it, but Saturday after Saturday he turned out, keeping up the pace and his form.

His moves were, and are, unpredictable. His somewhat angular form, topped by reddish hair, moves on a pair of legs which seem to jerk their way about the field, yet he has a swerve which is as graceful as a swallow's. Many footballers have mastered the feint back-heel, but Doherty prefers the forward feint. He pretends to kick the ball, checks his foot, and then darts away at an angle.

Where the ball is, you will find Doherty, but it goes even beyond that. Where the ball is going to be, he bobs up, with an unsurpassed flair for anticipating the ebb and flow of the game.

Manchester City played a Third Division side in a cup-tie, away from home, had a big share of the play, but could not score. They hammered away at their opponent's goal, when suddenly there was a break-away, the one danger to the crack side. The centre-half was out of position, the backs were all over the place. But there, running where the centre-half should have been, was Doherty. Single handed he stopped the breakaway, and City won through.

James played rarely for Scotland, Doherty often for Ireland. Ironically, he did not usually show his real form in these games, for even his genius was weighed down by the poverty of the material around him. And the supreme honour eluded him in 1947 when the Gt. Britain team was chosen to play the Rest of Europe in the match to celebrate the return of the home association to membership of F.I.F.A. The inside forwards were Steel and Mannion, with Carter in reserve.

But he had an afternoon of glory at Goodison Park in the autumn of the same year and in what seemed at the time must be the autumn of his career. Ireland drew 2-2 with England that day when a four or five goals win for the home country had generally been forecast. It was a fine game, and for once in a way Doherty, so often out of touch with the ball in these big games, found the rhythm to his liking. He was here, there, and everywhere, seeking the ball and using it. This was Doherty with the clock turned back, yet it seemed that even his efforts would be unavailing as the last seconds ran out and England led 2-1. But with the referee preparing to blow for time Doherty flung himself forward, headed the ball into the goal, and collapsed on the turf.

The professional manager, a little cold-bloodded in his appraisement of players and play, says of Doherty that he tries to do too much with the ball. Yet only a man in love with football, and longing to be in the thick of it, could have scored that goal.

Both James and Doherty played during the era when the stopper was becoming an essential part of every successful team, and when as a consequence more and more in the way of physical effort was expected of inside forwards, who had to draw back to fill the space left by the new defensive set-up but had to be able to do their share in attacking football. The strain on them, week by week, could have had one of two results. It could have shortened their careers, or it could have reduced their football to the hum-drum. It did neither, because both were men out of the ordinary.

It is impossible to say which was the finer inside forward in his great days. James was more of a character, more of a showman, and his skill at the long pass has been noted. Doherty preferred to flick a pass, as do the Continental artists, rather than to boot it across the full width of the field. Above all, he liked to be where the fun was fastest. He played with more spirit, more will to win than did James, whose interest in the proceedings was more concerned with the artistry of the game. In another chapter it has been laid down that one cannot say this or that fine player was better than another. Let's leave it that we are glad to have seen them both.

WIZARDS IN RED, WHITE, AND BLUE

Billy Meredith, Stanley Matthews,
and Alan Morton.

NO ONE has ever challenged the greatness of Billy
Meredith, Stanley Matthews, and Alan Morton. Of
all the fine wingers produced by Wales, England, and
Scotland, theirs are the outstanding names, and it is
interesting to record in passing that Ireland has turned
out nothing on the same level so far as wing positions
are concerned.

Billy Meredith, the senior of the three, came from
Chirk. He is said to have been recommended to
Manchester City by Mr. Lawrence Furness, who
afterwards became their chairman. At the time he
was a referee, and he thus enjoyed a close-up view of
the winger in a match between Chirk and Middlesbrough Ironopolis. But Mr. Furness would be the
last man to claim that he discovered Meredith, who
was there for all to see, sooner or later. It just
happened that the Manchester City man was there
sooner than the others.

Meredith played for City for some years, and then
when the trouble and the suspensions came, he went
to Manchester United. Ultimately he returned to
Manchester City, finishing his career in his fiftieth
year after gaining fifty-one international honours for
Wales and a Cup medal with each of his clubs.

For those who never saw Meredith play, it is difficult to build up a picture of his style. Old timers
are all agreed that he had genuine speed and fine
ball control, gained by hours of practice at dribbling
between stakes. They tell of his back-heel, delivered
at top speed and with uncanny accuracy, and of
course they mention his tooth-pick, which was often

a trimmed-down match-stick and which was, one should say for the sake of the record, an affectation not only of Meredith's but of most of the Manchester City players of that period.

Those with a clear memory who had an eye for technique are unanimous about these things, and they will tell you that the basis of his play was the run down the touch-line, which carried him right to the corner-flag, and the immaculate centre, fairly high but not without pace behind it to help the man heading it. The ball when centred was pulled back a yard or two, a method which prevented the inside forward from getting off-side and which also had the advantage of taking the ball away from the reach of the groping goalkeeper. This is a point worth noting by wingers who slavishly try to put centres and corner-kicks into the goalmouth with an in-swing, in the thousand-to-one hope of scoring direct. The normal kick should carry the ball away from goal as it swerves a little, and the in-swinger taken with the "wrong" foot reserved as a surprise-packet.

But when one has heard of these elements of Meredith's play, one comes up against a difficulty, and sharply, too. For Billy Meredith was a regular scorer of goals—and no man can score goals if he spends his football career in the yard segment by the corner-flag, as the Welshman is said to have done.

Figures of Meredith's goals vary because records were not so well kept in his early days and because he played in a lot of matches outside the normal run of the League fixtures, but even the lowest estimate puts the Meredih goals at around the two hundred mark. As against that it has been claimed that in the first part of his career alone, from 1894 until he left Manchester City in 1905, he scored two hundred and four golas. In 1898-99 he is said to have netted thirty-three times in thirty-six league games, an exploit surpassing even Bastin's well-authenticated feat of scoring thirty-three goals from outside left in forty-two games under a very different and more favourable off-side law. As soon as Meredith joined Manchester United his scoring ability seems to have declined, but at the end of his career Meredith himself claimed to have scored two hundred and eighty-one goals in eight hundred and fifty-seven League games, fifty-six goals in one hundred and sixty-six Cup-ties, fifteen in fifty-one International games, and one hundred and eighty goals in four hundred and ninety-four charity and friendly games, yielding a grand total of four hundred and seventy goals in one thousand five hundred and sixty-eight games, some of which, in cricket parlance would hardly rank as first-class.

It is true that Meredith was a regular and efficient penalty-kicker, but there must have been something else about his play to fashion him into a scoring winger with a deadly match-winning ability not surpassed by Jackson, Bastin, or Brook. And we must remember that he scored the important and controversial goal with which Manchester City beat Bolton Wanderers in the Cup Final at Crystal Palace. A picture of that game shows Meredith swerving to close in and shoot, and out of the old photograph comes an impression of a man with a raking stride and a dashing style which ill accords with the board-room gossip descriptive of his tram-line progress down the touch-line with extended elbows.

So there is the Meredith mystery, the trouble in harmonising the match-winner with the artist. But the difficulty of arriving at a true description of his style does not, fortunately, involve any belittlement of his overall prowess. A steward of the West Bromwich Albion club once engaged some journalists in conversation before a game at The Hawthorns, and when wingers were being talked about he named

Billy Bassett, then Athersmith, then Jocky Simpson and so on. Winger after winger came under the keen and enthusiastic examination of this old-timer. He had something good to say of each, one was fast, another tricky, and so on.

"And what about Meredith?" he was asked.

"Meredith? Oh, well, of course, he was the best of the lot, the daddy of the bunch," was the reply and he dismissed the Welshman without further discussion as though he was the complete winger. There were points for and against all the others, but Meredith called for no analysis.

Billy Meredith was, and is, a staunch supporter of the Players' Union, and is to be seen at their meetings, usually appointed to stand at the door to see that no unauthorised person gains admission. He does not smile often, and his general expression is critical; he seems to have little to say that is good of modern footballers. A lean man, a sort of Cassius among footballers his rivals might have said, but if such men are dangerous, his threat was only from his football. He must have been a scrupulously fair player himself or he would not have been able to play for thirty-one years with hardly an injury to interrupt his career.

With a special view to making a comparison between Meredith and Matthews, the question of their respective ability was put to two men: one sits in committee to assist in choosing England's international team, the other is an outstanding manager who was a first-class player in his youth.

The former said: "There has been only one Matthews, and I think we shall never see another."

The second man said scornfully: "Meredith was three times as good as Matthews."

There it is, and there can be no finality about it, any more than one can finish the old argument about Grace, Hobbs, and Bradman.

There is a mystery, too, about Stanley Matthews, and the puzzle in his case is this: had he set his heart on scoring goals, what could he have accomplished?

It is difficult to believe that there has ever been a footballer with such perfect technique. Completely two-footed, able with his superb speed to show any opponent a clean pair of heels, wonderfully balanced, tricky as a conjuror, he would appear to have the ability to run clean through a defence and pop the ball into the net. Yet except on rare occasions he has almost wilfully, so it seems, declined to acknowledge the old axiom that goals win matches. Can it be that Stanley Matthews, hailed at Stoke as The Wizard, is at heart the greatest democrat, and that he plays merely to entertain the man on the terraces? Or is he the Narcissus of the game, fatally enamoured with his own footwork?

When he was young he scored quite a few goals. One recalls an evening match at Stoke when the club were celebrating the opening of an extension to the covered accommodation. What a celebration it was! Stoke City over-ran Leeds United, and Matthews scored four times. He was irresistible that night. And there is the memory of that famous match when England played Czecho-Slovakia in London, and were almost beaten for the first time at home by Continental rivals. A man was hurt, the forward line had to be re-shaped, and Matthews found himslef at inside right, the position for which his great gifts seemed to mark him out but for which he never had any ambition. Three times he scored, each time with his left foot, and England won 5-4. The last goal, scored as the autumn mists fell over London, was the sort of thing you would think Stanley Matthews could do any Saturday afternoon, for he just picked up the ball, fastened it to his feet, and ran through half the other team before shooting.

I

About once in every other game Matthews heads the ball. Mostly he will do everything possible to avoid this. And yet you never see him head the ball but what he heads it perfectly, either nodding it forward so that he can run on to it, or steering it at just the angle he intends. On the stage, or in training, he can head the ball like a seal in a circus. Yet when play is on the left wing, and the orthodox move of the right winger is to close in, prepared to head a goal, you can count Matthews out of it. This is no part of the Matthews magic.

Matthews is the most modest of men, and it is difficult to persuade him to talk at length about himself or the game. After a match, when you go to congratulate him, he usually forestalls you with his: "Was it a good game to watch?" He has said that so often that one is almost assured that his first delight is to entertain the man who has paid to see the game . . . and to see Matthews.

His voice is so rarely raised that, were it not for a thousand photographs, he would be lost in any small crowd. He earns more than any other professional footballer—not from football as wages, but from other activities which include the hotel business, journalism, the stage, and adverstising. He dresses with a moderation amounting almost to parsimony. He is among the most happily married of men, has two children, works hard at anything he touches, is a non-drinker and non-smoker, and at the height of his fame trains as seriously and as keenly as when he was first learning the tricks (and what tricks!) of his trade.

When his time with Stoke City was coming to an end, and when all the world knew that a transfer was inevitable, the Blackpool manager had an appointment at Stoke to see officials of that club. Mr. Joe Smith asked Matthews, who was already living in Blackpool and training at Blomfield-road, if he would like to go with him and mentioned that he was setting out by car at about ten in the morning. Now at that particular time there was no disguising the lack of friendly feeling between Matthews and part of the Stoke officialdom, and to some of the public the player himself would have appeared to be under no particular obligation or necessity to maintain one hundred per cent loyalty to his first professional club. But he told Joe Smith: "I can't come. I have to train."

The son of a professional boxer, Matthews himself has related how he learned to keep fit when still a boy, how he was drilled in deep breathing exercises. He has never got out of that step.

For many years Matthews was notable, among other things, for the style in which he dribbled, keeping the ball in front of him; he seemed to take a delight in "showing" the ball to a back, as the players say, and then beating his man. But about the time he moved to Blackpool he also adopted the trick of shielding the ball with his body, compelling an opponent to delay his tackle or to risk fouling. About the same time he seemed to become more eager to go searching for the ball.

His standard method of beating a man is so well known that one can only marvel that it has not been more widely copied. Up to the back with the ball, a wriggle of the backside as the defender hesitates, a switch from foot to foot, and then a sudden spurt— perhaps the finest acceleration the game has known. There was never a player who could trap the ball better than Matthews—stone dead it drops at his feet, the hardest pass at longest range brought instantly under control.

It took Matthews a long time to live down the Italian match of 1934—the Battle of Highbury as it is called to this day. It was a rough match with the Italians—on the field and sitting in the stand—in a frenzy, and some of the English players were compelled to answer back in self-preservation. The right wing of Bowden and Matthews was not suited to this kind of thing and they played little part in England's win, which was doubtful for a time but emphatic in the end. But Matthews got back after a year in the wilderness, and in 1938 played possibly his finest game when he tore the Irish defence to ribbons at Old Trafford and presented Willie Hall with five goals.

Towards the end of that game he ran clean through the Irish team and scored one for himself. The gesture was unmistakable; it was as clear as could be that Matthews, having played as a loyal team-man and provided openings for inferior players, and having done it all in the most artistic way, decided to take one for Matthews.

It was that day, too, that the late William Parkinson decided that Matthews should play for Blackpool one day. It took several years for the fulfilment of the dream.

During the war years Matthews' R.A.F. postings permitted him to play a good deal of football, some of it not very serious, much quite light-hearted, and his reputation continued to expand. Then after the war his final fall-out with Stoke took him to Blackpool, but not before he had played for Great Britain against the Rest of Europe at Hampden Park. It was soon after this that criticism of Matthews the footballer began to be heard. Someone or other struck a bright line by saying or writing that he slowed up the other forwards, and it was taken up as a parrot-cry. Selected to play in Ireland, he dropped out through injury and Finney, who took his place, did so well that the older man's place in the side was seriously threatened. Matthews came back to the team, but no longer was his position by his right. It was one of football's most interesting topics for discussion: Finney or

Matthews? Unfortunately the argument was not carried on coolly or intelligently.

It is perhaps not known to many that Matthew's goal-scoring possibilities were considered by Walter Winterbottom, when that fine student of the game became England's team-manager. At a time when the winger had apparently decided that entertainment or pure football was his role, he was persuaded by Winterbottom that his beautiful footwork was not inconsistent with shooting.

So in one international match he came to the front as a marksman, and there were four tremendous shots; one at least would have gone into the net but for the fact that one of his colleagues, with more zeal than judgment, decided to help the ball in . . . and helped it out.

It is unlikely that Matthews will play until he his fifty, as Meredith did, but that will probably be only because he just does not want to. Like the Welshman, he has remained remarkably free from injury and in his middle thirties he has retained so much of his skill and speed that he looks practically as good as ever. One of the reasons for his freedom from injury is his own sportsmanlike method of play; no one has ever seen him guilty of a petty act on the field of play. Another reason is his superb sense of balance. That has been his insurance policy.

The third of these three M's, Alan Morton, never played in English football. His reputation in England therefore depends on the Scottish estimate of his prowess and on what he did in international matches. Of his stature, however, there can be no doubt. He played for Scotland thirty times against England, Wales, and Ireland between 1920 and 1932 and his reputation in that time was the equal of the reputation Matthews was to make. Our selectors had to find a man to stop Morton, just as Scotland later had the problem of finding a back to stand up to Matthews. These were vintage years for Scottish football, including the 1926 Wembley Wizzards, and usually Scotland had the better of their games against England, with Morton the brightest of all the stars.

Like Matthews and Meredith, he has left behind a memory of a player with a beautiful action, who seemed never to be caught out in an untidy attitude, never sprawling when bringing the ball under control. Possibly he had fewer tricks, less variety in his play, than either of the others, but his balance, his confidence which amounted almost to cheek, enabled him to master every back pitted against him. In any gallery of famous players, Morton, the Wee Blue Devil, must be there no less than Meredith or Matthews.

CONSTRUCTIVE DEFENDERS

Stanley Cullis, Frank Swift,
and Johnny Carey.

WITH ALL the authority that he possesses from his brilliant playing career and his experience as a manager, Matt Busby declares that the one outstanding improvement in football during his time has been in constructive defence. And anyone who has watched football over the period covered by Busby's career— from, say, 1929 to the present day—will readily agree. With one or two brilliant exceptions, wing play has deteriorated; inside forward play is stereotyped; centre-forwards are held in the grip of the stopper; wing half backs have become keystones in the arch of defence, instructed to pin down their opponents. But full-backs, goalkeepers, and one or two centre-half backs have shown how attacks can be marshalled and developed from the rear.

It is as though, in the midst of a war, trench warfare, the close conflict of masses of men, had brought temporary stalemate. Minds got to work to produce the tank; then the longer-range weapons of the second world war. Football is a battle, and at the present time the long-range attack, thoughtfully prepared at base, is proving an effective weapon and a pleasing spectacle.

As the twentieth century moved into its early 30's, football became dominated by the stopper centre-half and his attendant evils of pulled-in wing-halves. Preventing goals became for a time the principal preoccupation of players and managers. The centre-half back, once the most gloriously free player on the side permitted to wander in attack and defence as the ebb and flow of the game suggested, retreated until he became a third back. Indeed, it is hard to understand why the phrase " centre-half " has persisted in British football. On the Continent they have already begun to print his name on a level with the two full-backs of tradition, and it would seem to present an opening for some ambitious club, eager for attention, to re-number its players. Logically, if the right-back is " 2 ", the centre-half or stopper should be " 3 " and the left-back " 4 ", with the wing-halves " 5 " and " 6 ". But that is by the way.

As the stopper established himself, a new problem emerged. He had solved the one of stopping the centre-forward from scoring goals, and he had haps gone a long way from scoring goals, and he had perhaps gone a long way towards mastering the problem of securing the ball. But the new problem which urgently presented itself was: what was he to do with the ball? It was all very well banging it away as quickly as you drop a hot chestnut back into the hearth on a winter's evening, all very well heading the ball up-field with thick-skulled energy. But the ball had a nasty habit of coming back to you, and continually coming back, and you found yourself engaged in a never-ending defensive struggle which was wearying and profitless.

So the new problem was this: how to stay back in the third-back position and yet usefully dispose of the ball? Some centre-half backs hardly bothered to put their heads to the question, preferring to play with a camel-like intelligence and destructive prowess which satisfied some managers, some of the public, but none who had the interests of soccer at heart.

One of the first men to attempt to break out of the line of camels travelling nose to tail along their por-fessional careers was Barker of Derby County. Jack Barker was a fairly heavy man, not particularly graceful, and he could tackle in the best Derby fashion. So frills were not for him, but he did develop a slashing kick to the wings which enabled his team to burst away from a defending position with fast, effective raids towards the other goal. The method was good enough so far as it went, for it shifted the game quickly—generally agreed as a desirable feature before the full import of the new off-side law was understood—but with a pass to be made up to half the length of the field, there was considerable scope for error.

Into the football scene stepped Stanley Cullis. He became a Wolverhampton Wanderers player as a boy, was carefully coached under Frank Buckley's stern regime, and showed such gifts, not merely as a footballer but as a leader, that he impressed his own club's officials as a probable captain of England even before he had figured in a first-class match.

Cullis had courage. He was not afraid to stop the ball in the heart of the game in his own penalty-area, and he never hesitated to attempt to beat a man to give himself more room for his clearance-kick. His style was not flawless for although he was light on his feet, he had a habit of crouching as though shielding the ball from some would-be marauder, and he tended to stick his elbows out.

Able to trick a man, Cullis could make a little ground and then deliver a short pass to a wing-half or an inside forward, and it was this perfection of football which made him such an outstanding figure in the years immediately before the second war.

One would hesitate to describe his first appearance for England as a triumph. Although he was opposed by a shortish centre-forward, he frequently failed to gain the mastery of his rival when the ball was in the air and now and again, in the thick of things, he seemed to take his eye off the ball and to be brushed aside too easily. But Cullis had the will and the ability to learn, and it took him only a little while to put the finishing touches to his method of play. His appearance in the England team had been awaited with interest, for he followed Alf Young, the complete and absolute stopper. His partial failure in Ireland was forgiven by wise selectors (and may one add, imaginative journalists?) and there he stayed.

His early tendency to be knocked to one side in the bustle of meeting a high ball was so completely mastered that it was his ability to meet just such a situation that was given by Cliff Britton as the reason why " Stanley is the centre-half for me ".

Britton said of Cullis: " He took an awful lot of knocks. Forwards who knew he wanted to stop the ball and hold it went barging in, hoping to rattle him. A high ball would come over, and as it hung a little in the air with Cullis waiting to head it to a teammate or try to nod it down for himself, a centre-forward would tear in, making for ball and man and perhaps hoping most to take the man. Cullis would take the ball, and perhaps be bowled over . . . or worse. A minute later the incident might be repeated. Over would come the ball, it would hang in the air, and Cullis knew that someone was waiting to have a go at him. But he would glue his eye on the ball, and ignore the risk of another hurtful challenge. For him, it was the ball all the time. He took a lot of punishment, but it was always the ball. That's why he will always remain, for me, the one centre-half."

About the same time that Cullis was establishing himself at Wolverhampton, Manchester City had a strapping young goalkeeper named Frank Swift. It is hard to say exactly what position he should occupy in the list of great footballers in this position, because he did not gain a cap before the war and only won his place in the English team during the war years and after. But in one branch of football he claims a secure place in history, for he showed goalkeepers all over the world the way they could become team-men.

Just as Cullis was foreshadowed by Barker, Swift had a forerunner in Holdcroft of Preston North End, whose advances to the edge of the penalty area frequently made him into an extra back. Swift worked on different lines. A big man, with a powerful dead-ball kick, he was soon struck by the futility of lunging the ball over the half-wayline for an opponent to head back. The scrambling for points in League matches does not encourage experiments, and it may be that Swift only really had a chance to put his ideas into practice in the somewhat slower, less competitive, games of the war years when he played alongside and against footballers of all grades. Certainly it was not until full-scale football was resumed in 1946 that Swift emerged as the complete team-man, able to use the ball. It was, like all good ideas, simple in its conception. Having obtained the ball, he had to give it a team-mate, and for this purposce Frank Swift employed several devices. The most spectacular was the long drop-kick, which he mastered to such an extent that in one match he was able to land the ball at Matthews' feet half-a-dozen times, the ball flying low and truly like a well-hit golf-drive. Another method, made possible only by his great physical strength, was the development of the long throw, a trick which brought guffaws of amusement and roars of applause on every ground where he played.

Swift's disposal of the ball reached its limits of efficiency when he shortened his aim and learned to co-operate with the full backs. It is possible that consciously or otherwise he picked up some hints from the famed Manchester City pair, Barkas and Bray, who, just before the war in the club's League championship season, had shown what could be done by intelligent running into position even on the fringe of their own penalty area. There came a time when Swift, playing in international football and therefore with the best and most intelligent players available for the exploitation of such tricks, found that he could hold the ball while a full-back made ground into an open space, and then throw him the ball. This move had an instantaneous effect on full-back play, too: Aston, of Manchester United, soon had his own club goalkeeper, an average First Division player, doing the same thing, and to see Aston run away from the goalmouth, wait for the ball, collect it, and start an attack remains one of the happiest features of his team's brilliant play.

But if Aston is a fine back, quick to learn a move, slow to forget an experience, able to profit by all he sees, what is to be said of that prince of full-backs, his club-mate and captain John Carey? The finest of all full-backs in the immediate post-war period, Carey was described by Cullis as " THE BRAIN of football. I only wish I could have played with him for a couple of years."

Carey began his footballing life as an inside forward and there seemed a chance that he might make a second Peter Doherty. But there was a difference somewhere, perhaps that between an instinctive player and a thoughtful one. So Carey moved to the half-back line, to full-back, in fact almost anywhere to suit the needs of his side. He was a wing-half and captain in The Rest of Europe team which came to Britain to celebrate the patching up of the F.I.F.A. squabble, but by the time Manchester United won the Cup in 1948 he was well established as the premier full-back.

He has most of the virtues that go to make up a great back; here we are concerned with his kicking. Like Cullis, Carey prefers to take risks rather than slap the ball up the field in a hurry or to kick out of play. He beats a man in much the same way as Cullis, crouching a little, using the side of the boot and a rubber-like twist of the hips.

Some players need to wind themselves up to kick. They require anything from a few inches to several feet of spare space to set themselves for the blow, just as some boxers need to set themselves for a punch. Not Carey; once he has made his decision to kick, he seems able to shift the ball with a minimum of effort, appearing sometimes—to use a golfing simile—to cut it up like a golfer with a restricted swing.

How good were Crompton and Pennington? Very good, without any doubt, and it is no purpose of this chapter to belittle those or any other footballers of a by-gone age. Crompton's stooping tackle and kicking up the side-line must have been marvels of athletic prowess. But watching Carey it is difficult to imagine that any full-back in the long history of the game has had a greater comprehension of the job.

Think what it means to an inside forward when a full-back hurriedly bangs the ball into touch deep in his own half. There is a throw-in for which the wing-halves must position themselves (one for the throw, one to cover the centre), and for which the inside for-wards, already weary with their perpetual motion to and fro, must therefore come back. Every yard they trot is a little chunk chipped off their playing careers, a toll taken of flesh and blood. Carey's method saves that. The inside forwards who play with him have their football lives prolonged by the sheer beauty of his footballing method.

There was a time in 1949 when Manchester United looked like being faced with a centre-half problem. Chilton had indicated a desire to leave the club, and it was not certain that Lynn could do the job. He did for a few weeks, and did it very well, and then Chilton changed his mind and returned to the team.

Meantime Matt Busby had Carey, still playing at full-back, as his stand-by choice for centre-half.

It was a happy ending, from Manchester United's point of view, when Chilton slipped back into the side, playing better than ever before. But from another angle, one may reflect and regret, a prolonged spell at centre-half by Carey might have given the game a new glory and a new conception of what a centre-half could accomplish within the frame-work of the modern off-side law. A better first-time kicker than Cullis, and probably better at long-range work, Carey seems the one man who might have carried on where the Wolverhampton man left off. Maybe he would not have revelled in the close-quarter rough and tumble, maybe there would have been too much artistry and insufficient ruthlessness in clearing attacks. One can only ponder and sigh at a missed opportunity . . . for the spectators. Football from the Press Box can be awfully dull, one match looking very like another. Nice to have been presented with a new spectacle!

NO CHASE TOO HARD

Like Denis Compton,
they played all the year round.

EVER since W. G. Grace interrupted an innings at
the Oval to go the running track and win the hurdles
championship of England, the all-rounder has been
much admired. A particular reverence is accorded
such a man as C. B. Fry, who played for England at
cricket and was captain, too; gained an international
soccer cap; held the world's long jump record; missed
a rugby Blue only through injury; and indeed seemed
capable of almost anything. Or such another as Max
Woosnam, who made a hundred for the Public
Schools at Lord's; played alongside professional footballers and was capped for England; and contrived,
too, to be a doubles champion at Wimbledon. A new
man of the same breed is Hubert Doggart, five times
a Cambridge Blue, and at the time of writing one of
his country's greatest cricket hopes for the future.

Many of the early soccer stars were all-rounders,
and indeed the link between cricket and Association
football, as instance the playing of early Cup Finals
on the ground which was to stage the first Test
match, is a firm one. As one studies the invasion of
professionalism into both games, and as overseas
tours became a commonplace, one would anticipate
specialisation such as is generally adopted in the
United States. Yet there has never been any failure
in the steady stream of men possessing not merely
the ambition to play for England at two games, but
the driving energy to play top-class stuff all the year
round.

The true double international is, of course, a rare
bird. Two wars have made it possible for various

footballers and cricketers to achieve substitute honours, but the real thing, the two caps won when selectors had a free choice, is not often gained. In fact in the year 1950 there is only one man still playing football and cricket who can claim that in peacetime he turned out for England at both games. He is John Arnold, of Fulham at soccer and of Hampshire at cricket, and even in his case he never appeared against Australia and at neither game was he able to achieve continuous representative selection.

William Gunn was one of the first double internationals, and it seems that he fairly won his honour at both games. He was a soccer forward, and as he stood 6ft. 3ins., and is described as very skilful and very fast, he must have taken some stopping. Has a taller man ever played for England at football, by the way—at any rate in the forward line?

This cannot pretend to be a catalogue of all the double internationals, but on scanning the names one or two stand out clearly: R. E. Foster, for instance, whose record score in an Anglo-Australian Test match stood for so long and who was first-class at rackets and golf as well as soccer, at which he gained five international caps at the turn of the century. Cricket's sweetest honour, the captaincy of a team to travel to Australia, was offered him, claims of business compelled him to turn it down, and the opportunity did not occur again.

Harry Makepeace played for England often enough at soccer to make a great name for himself as a half-back between the years 1906 and 1912, and he was in Everton's Cup-winning side. From knowing the man and his cricket, one may guess that he was a severely practical player relying on the application of a correct method.

His cricket prowess took him to Australia and to the fulfillment of every player's ambition, a century

in a Test match; later on, after many seasons of valued work in the field for Lancashire, he became their senior coach at Old Trafford. Many cricketers and footballers, and not a few journalists, have reason to be grateful to him for kindly advice.

Harry Makepeace was right-half in that Everton Cup-winning team, and in front of him on the right wing was Jack Sharp, already an international and destined to play for England in Test matches. His career at both games was so brilliant that even the sober Wisden's described it as unparralleled. He played in both of Everton's Cup Finals of his time, and on the only two occasions he played for England was on the winning side. He scored a century against Australia (the only one for England in that particular series) and after playing as a professional, turned amateur and captained Lancashire. And then when his playing days were over he became a director of the Everton club and served on the Test match Selection Committee, so there was reason for Wisden's superlative.

There was Andy Ducat of Surrey and Aston Villa. On the soccer field he missed a Cup Final through injury, his deputy scoring the winning goal, but after the interruption of a war Aston Villa reached the Final again—and Ducat was there to crown his career with a winner's medal. Walter Hardinge (who was pretty-well ambidextrous) was another double international, and so was L. H. Gay.

Two of the greatest batsmen ever possessed by Middlesex, Patsy Hendren and Denis Compton, played for England at cricket by right of their outstanding talent, and both won substitute soccer honours. Compton's career is still fresh in mind; as a footballer he possibly owed something to his name as a cricketer, but he had a flair for the big occasion, and the crowds loved him. His soccer exploits were

K

dramatically rounded off for the Arsenal outside-left with a Cup-winner's medal only a week or two before the revelation of the gravity of the knee injury which finished his football for good and so seriously threatened his cricket.

These are some of the most famous, the men who have climbed to the top; but there have been and are many men who have played both games consistently well and with substantial reward to their pockets.

A Compton with his five-figure cricket benefit and his soccer bonuses is of course an exception but there are up and down England many gamesmen who have never gained international honours, and never will, who are making a very good thing out of sport. Some professional footballers figure regularly in county cricket; others play in league cricket and at the summer game achieve local esteem in lieu of national fame . . . but it all helps. After all, if a man is receiving something between six and ten pounds a week from a football club in summer pay, just for maintaining his contract with a club who thus retain his signature and transfer rights, anything extra from cricket, whether it be a fiver a week from an obscure league club or a thousand a year and a tax-free benefit from cricket of Test standard, is putting him in to bat on what is financially a very good wicket.

The physical strain is great. Only this year Compton's knee—headlined, photographed, cartooned—was a reminder that in chasing a ball for twelve months in the year the human frame is exposed to some risk of breaking down.

Yet on the other hand many men, perhaps blessed with extra stamina and strength, or maybe happy in some knack of being able to conserve their energies by economy or grace of movement, keep going to enjoy long careers at both games.

The complete all-the-year-rounder is, as has already

been noted, a rare bird. Usually the man who gains both international caps only scrambles the honour at one of them.

Harry Makepeace was one of the modern exceptions because he really won his way to international class at both games and earned his soccer caps equally with his trip to Australia where he became the first man to spot Arthur Mailey's googly with any certainty. As, like Jack Sharp, he played in both of everton's Cup Finals in successive seasons, tasting both victory and defeat, he should know all about the effect of a big match on a man's nerves, and he was in no doubt about his answer when asked about the relative impact on a man's temperament of a Test match and a Cup Final.

After seeing men in the dressing-room at Crystal Palace literally sick with apprehension, and unable to lace up their boots, he still thought a Test match was the greater strain. At football, there are eleven men playing together and they can talk—even shout—to one another. The nervous man can be pulled along by the others by cajolery, by jollying, by gentle bullying. In a game of movement, such as soccer, he can be swept along by the game, carried out of himself. But at cricket, you largely stand on your own feet. The quiet of the walk to wicket, the hush which awaits the bowling of the first ball in a Test match (was there anything more remarkable in cricket than the stillness of the crowd as Larwood ran to bowl?) —no one can help the batsman or the bowler in that moment.

W. G. himself summed it all up when he gave the kindly reply to the fluttering female who asked him if he wasn't nervous when he was batting, when he thought of all that depended on him and the possible end of his innings:

"Madam, there is nothing worse to think about than the next ball to be bowled."

And of course a Test match lasts longer than a foot-ball match with its "ninety minutes of concentrated excitement" in Pardon's rather scornful phrase. The Cup Final has its weeks of waiting, it is true, those days and weeks during which every friend wants a ticket and everyone who wants a ticket becomes the player's friend; but a Test match, once started, still has its five or six days and wakeful nights.

Anyway, Makepeace should know, and he puts the Test match an easy first for its fraying of the nerves. These things react in differing ways on different men. Did not Denis Compton sleep in the dressing-room before he went to bat in a Test? And did not Stanley Mortensen sleep in the coach on the way to Villa Park immediately before he accomplished the great-est of all his scoring feats? And on the contrary, did not one fine cricketer (and a fine man, too) make such a hash of his opening over that he told his friends that he had wished Old Trafford would open up and swallow him?

Sometimes there is a clash of interests for these cricketing-footballers. The seasons overlap, and so do the claims of their employers. Prior date of a con-tract may decide the tug-o'-war, more usually there is friendly agreement. For instance, Willie Watson of Yorkshire and Sunderland was already a Test trial-ist and therefore was entitled to have high aims at cricket when he was chosen to play football for Eng-land against Italy in the late autumn of 1950. It became apparent that ultimately he would be in the running for a football trip to Rio. Yorkshire told him that the issue would be left to him, and in due course, when the Football Association issued their invitation, he elected to play soccer in June and July, forfeiting his place in the Yorkshire team, then brilliantly win-ning it back in August.

Already Yorkshire and Sunderland had shown the

way for other clubs in agreeing on the share they would take of Watson's services: In the late summer of 1959 Yorkshire were bidding for the cricket championship, so the player stayed with them and took part in that memorable finish when a two-day win over Glamorgan enabled them to share the title with Middlesex. Similarly the following spring, with Sunderland hoping to win the Football League championship, Watson stayed on to the end instead of starting the season with Yorkshire. A realistic view; the club most in need of his services, enjoyed them.

Many years before, Compton had taken the contrary view to Watson's, and stuck to the game for the season. In 1938-39 he could have gone to South Africa with Hammond's team, but he preferred to stay at home with Arsenal.

A special place in history is reserved for Gordon Hodgson and Ken Grieves. Both came from overseas to play here—Hodgson soccer with Liverpool, Grieves cricket in the Lancashire League. Hodgson won soccer caps for England, and as a side-line played league and county cricket; he was a fast bowler of enthusiasm and strength if lacking something of the fire and artistry which makes a man into a Test bowler. Grieves, a magnificent cricket all-rounder, joined Bury as a goalkeeper.

These all-rounders are among the most interesting of games players. To the ordinary mortal, who finds one game difficult enough, they are the gods of games, and he can only marvel at the prodigality of Nature which has given these men that little extra something so that no day can be too long, no chase too hard.

THE MAN WITH THE SPONGE

Seven days a week,
but never a headline.

THE trainer's story may best be started with a tale from real life. Sometime in the late 'twenties a boy of fifteen, by name of William Ridding, signed amateur forms for Tranmere Rovers, a Third Division club which in quick succession had produced two crack centre-forwards in Dean and Waring, both destined to play for England. Young Ridding was a centre-forward, too, and within a year he was not merely taking part in the hurly-burly of League football, but was looking almost as good as the two famous men who had preceded him. It looked as though Tranmere had done it again. In due course Ridding went to Manchester City, then to their neighbours the United at Old Trafford. At the age of 24, in all the glory of his young manhood, he received a knee injury which finished his active football for good.

Unless he is an exceptional case, a young man who has been living football for nine years from the age of fifteen is not particularly well qualified to face the world minus his boots. Ridding knew he would eventually get some compensation for his injury, but that would take time.

The next two years tested his character. He had to learn a new trade, and he decided to stay in the game as a trainer. He went to Liverpool, slaved away at his lessons, rode the rough tide, and went back to Tranmere in the lowly post of third team trainer. After sundry promotions and experiences he migrated to Bolton Wanderers, as senior trainer to a First Division club. Within four years he was given a chance to look after a representative side.

Then he went on a Football Association tour to the Continent. He was watched for ten days by the F.A. officials, perhaps more closely than they observed even the players, to see if he would " do ". He did all right, and was given the trainer's supreme honour of taking the team to Rio to play in the World Cup.

Now a man does not get to the top of any job without some kind of quality in his personal make-up. If you see Ridding at a League match on a Saturday afternoon he will be wearing a wind-cheater zipper jacket and will carry a little bag. He may only be on the field once or twice, and it is long odds that each time he will produce a sponge from which cold water (and this may be in December or February) will be dashed over a player's head or squelched down his neck. A seemingly brutal form of reviver from which many a player has recoiled as the icy drops lashed his bare skin.

If you think that is the beginning and end of a trainer's job, you are as mistaken as though you believe that a Test batsman has done his job when he bought a new bat, or a novelist written a book when he has put paper in his typewriter.

It is well known that a football manager must be something of a psychologist. The trainer must be all of one. The manager, by the very title of his job, is on the employers' side of the fence. The trainer is in the dressing room with the players and is the link between the two parties. It is he who has to keep confidences of both club and men, and who should know when they must be shared. It is he who must know whether a young player has the delicate nervous fibre which calls for coaxing, or is of the rough-hewn stuff which will respond best to a little well-judged hectoring. He must know which player likes his occasional pint of beer, and which man

makes it more than an occasional one, if there should
be a black sheep in his flock. He must know which
youthful professional is smoking too much, and how
to persuade him to cut down. He may even find it
necessary to drop a hint to the eighteen-year old who,
flushed with easy success and unaccustomed earnings,
is spending too much money with his tailor.

He is responsible for the players' kit and its
laundering. He helps the manager in all sorts of
small ways, even in office work. When the manager,
his immediate superior, is worried beyond sleep over
the non-success of the team or some of it, he is the
one who lends the sympathetic ear to the unfortunate
boss's tale of trouble.

The trainer will handle many men with injuries
grave and small. For each there must be the correct
treatment and if necessary the calling in of a surgeon
or doctor. And if the medical man talks, as medical
men will, in the jargon of the profession, the trainer
must be sufficiently learned to understand what it is
all about so that the prescribed treatment may be
given.

Some players are " babies ". They require coaxing
when they have been hurt, require kidding just a little
before they come into action again. There will be
occasions when the trainer's hands, feeling their way
over an injured limb, will be as sympathetic as a
musician's. At other times they will kneed and
pound, bringing tears to the eyes of the patient, but
in either case bringing ease from pain and fitness to
play football again.

Some trainers have a knack of jollying their men
along. Some are quiet and by their very reserve in-
spire confidence. Some, the rare ones, have the knack
of being grave or gay to suit the occasion and such a
one, if he has technical skill, too, is a pearl beyond
price.

The forty-hour week is unknown to members of this profession. On Sunday morning they sort kit, attend to injuries from the previous day's play . . and then work non-stop until the following Saturday evening when, if you are on a train, you may perhaps see a team travelling home from an away match, with a game or two of cards in session, perhaps a little community singing, but at one end of the coach there will be the trainer, hands busy, giving first-aid to a player with a toe-nail pushed back or making up a list of drinks, or talking to the manager about so-and-so's domestic problem which may call for a week's leave in Scotland, or telling a player how to apply that cold compress when he reaches home, or maybe even advising that young professional, fair-haired, bright-eyed, and loving life, never to lead from his Ace-Queen.

During the week there are practice balls to be inflated, more kit to be watched, players to see, even homes to be visited. Medical appliances to be checked and kept up to stock level, sun-ray lamps to be used with the judgment, perhaps a tip to the manager that a second-team youth, of whom good reports are coming in, is justifying them at practice. If there is a mid-week international match, there is perhaps an excursion for the players to be organized, a decision as to whether an injured player should stay at home or travel with " the lads " to see the big game.

You have all seen the little bag and the sponge, but that is only part of the miscellany of equipment. There is a bigger outfit, a suit-case which goes to away matches, with bottles and bandages and odd things valued at a hundred pounds or more. Inside the dressing-rooms there is the electrical apparatus, the rowing machine, all the equipment of a pocket gymnasium.

Able to talk football with players, press, manager

and directors, all on level terms; a psychologist; a father and mother in one; a bit of a doctor, a bit of a chemist, the whole of masseur; a man's man; a good mixer; a good talker when its necessary, equally good at listening; not just an organizer, but a fixer; willing to subjugate himself to the back row, ready to jump into the forefront of action. That's the perfect trainer, and if he doesn't make a perfect husband too, that must be the wife's fault!

And all for what? Having acquired from Nature and by training and experience these manifold virtues, a first-class trainer will earn about the same weekly wage as a maximum-wage professional player. He will not rank for the five-yearly benefit, but he may receive a gift if one of the game's big prizes—a championship or a Cup Final appearance—is won. He will almost certainly be " on " the same bonus as the players week by week, two pounds for a win and a pound for a draw—because the club regard him as a player's man, as much part of the dressing-room as the men who kick the ball about.

His financial reward is not great, therefore; but if his health is good he may look forward to carrying on for many years, certainly into late middle age and perhaps longer if sight and hearing serve him well. His chief reward must be that which comes from service, for the good trainer is the beloved physician.

PART THREE

Great
Occasions

by

BOTH OF US

THESE CLUBS YOU HAVE LOVED

The game changes
but the tradition lingers on.

WHAT IS IT in football that makes a citizen who for six days of the week pursues normal respectability, suddenly for a few hours on Saturday afternoon decide to make him black his face, wear a battered or gaily-coloured top-hat, festoon himself with favours of one kind or another, delight in shouting himself hoarse, or sound a noisome rattle or bell? Is it a throw-back to the day when the Ancient Briton daubed on woad, is it another method of putting on the war-paint before battle, or is it that there must be a jester with his cap and bells at every court?

Certain it is that all this lusty expression and enthusiasm was born just about the same time as professionalism. The one seemed naturally to follow the other. Soccer suddenly passed from a cultured, privileged coterie to the masses, who laid a great paw on the game, looked at it, and loved it.

It is also fairly certain that most of this burlesque originated in the robust North, for when Blackburn Rovers went to play Queen's Park (yes, the Scottish amateurs) in the Cup Final of 1884 at Kennington Oval, London was invested by enthusiasts whom the 'Pall Mall Gazette' described as "a Northern horde of uncouth garb and strange oaths," and went on further to liken them to a tribe of Sudanese Arabs let loose. Each year now, London takes a delight in following the same theme if a Northern team is in the Final—conveniently forgetting that Southern "fans" are just as boisterous and colourful in invading Northern fastnesses.

But there is something rather more to it all than just dressing up. Partisanship, whether it brings joy or sorrow, is probably the greatest reason—love of a club, its players, its achievements (real and potential), the pleasure in a great performance, the despair in a dismal defeat. Is there a man whose heart throbs within him who cannot be moved by these things?

Love of a club . . . Dreams of the present, the middle past, and the distant beginning . . . Memories . . . Tradition. . . . Yes, the game may have changed, but the melody lingers on. . . .

Tradition. It is always of the past and yet is created in the present. For instance, those old-timers who have likened the Manchester United of modern times to that of the days of Duckworth, Roberts, Bell and Meredith, probably have not even considered the prospect of the younger enthusiasts of to-day comparing some future United team to that of Carey, Aston, Rowley, and Mitten. So it goes on—comparison, discussion, argument, from the individual dashing, dribbling days of the Wanderers, through the short-passing style first popularised by such teams as Blackburn Rovers, Preston North End, Aston Villa, and others, to the present period of attack based upon defence. What next? No one knows. The older ones, with nostalgic memories of what has gone before, would like to turn back the pages; younger ones would prefer to flick them over to the lightning speed of the Italians and Brazilians.

Ivan Sharpe once put into a sentence of six words the greatest reason for the popularity of the game: "All the World loves a goal." It is one of the finest sentences ever written about the game. It epitomises everything. You can have the greatest game in history, but without a goal, the crowd feels that it has missed something. If you just wanted football for the sake of movement, you might as well take away the goalposts. And without the goalposts there would be little or no movement. The goal is the ultimate of whatever type of play you like or dislike. The winning teams are the ones who are most remembered. They are the ones who have built up and who will continue to build up this thing called tradition.

When Soccer became an organised game 80 years ago, the Wanderers more than anyone of their time— more than the Royal Engineers, Old Etonians, Oxford University, Clapham Rovers, or any of the others— created a standard which will serve as an example for as long as Soccer is played. Their record of three consecutive Cup triumphs as well as other things in those far-off days has been equalled once, but never beaten. Their mode of play would be completely futile to-day, but the early efforts of those public-school and university " types " created an ideal for all those clubs who were to follow.

What tremendous changes the game has since experienced! How important it is in the lives of millions of people—even the latest intimation from Colombia is that the rapid growth of Soccer in that Central American republic with its introduction of English players, is welcomed by the Government to counteract political turbulence! How that would open the eyes in amazement of those handful of men who first decided to formulate a few rules and so establish a great sport.

How different from the times when Old Etonians contributed £5 to the expenses of their opponents, Darwen, so that the little Lancashire side could go back to The Oval to contest a Cup replay in 1879!

So from Wanderers and others with their undying amateur tradition, to the first of the great professional teams, Blackburn Rovers. Yet it might be wondered what Rovers' history might have been had the ground of Blackburn Olympic at Hole-i'-the-Wall not been situated a little too far out of town for the liking of those early football fans. Olympic created history by being the first club to take the Cup from the South. They were the first team to go into special Cup training. Composed of weavers, spinners, a picture-framer, an iron-moulder's dresser, a dentist's assistant, and so on, their average height was only 5ft. 6ins.—their opponents in that Final of 1883, Old Etonians, were two or three inches taller. Their supporters, many wearing their Sunday clogs with brass rivets, and scarves and neckties in the club colours, created a sensation in London, where the Cup never returned for another 20 years. Olympic's homecoming set the standard for the return of every Cup-winning team to follow. Their wagonette, drawn by six horses, was preceded through Blackburn by six brass bands.

The next year, the Cup was back again in Blackburn—and in each of two more years to follow: four times in all. Rovers took over where Olympic left off to equal the three-times-in-succession triumph of the Wanderers. Blackburn Rovers with their professionalism were a power in the land. That was when such men as H. J. Arthur, F. Suter, H. McIntyre, J. H. Forrest, J. Douglas, J. Sowerbutts, and J. Brown largely carried all before them—except the League championship, which they did not win until 1912.

Left half Forrest altogether won five Cup medals with Rovers—three in succession in the years from 1884-1886, and two in succession in 1890 and 1891. So from the pomp of those early days have Blackburn's elite battled through the decades to enjoy a Cup record that equals Aston Villa's six victories, but alas! how their circumstance has altered. Luck runs in cycles, however, and it is hoped that one day we will see the Rovers recapturing all their old skill and re-establishing themselves high in favour again.

There are clubs who should never fade—Preston North End as much as Blackburn. Proud Preston, The Invincibles who went through that 1888-89 season without a defeat in the League and without conceding a goal in the Cup—a feat that still stands alone. People spoke of them with bated breath. Each and everyone of them subordinated his own interests to that of the side. Mr. R. Sudell, the chairman of those days, saw to that.

Sudell had a modern counterpart in Mr. James Taylor, a man also of quite decided views, but one of the most knowledgeable and deeply respected in the game. One helped to build up the tradition and the other strove might and main to preserve it in an age when good forward play tottered against the bastion of the third-back game. Jim Taylor has now retired from the club chairmanship, is now life-president of the club. He lives as Sudell lived before him —for Preston North End. Singularly, Preston have never been able to win the League championship since they carried it off in the first two years it was first introduced. Tom Finney, local plumber and England's greatest outside right after Stanley Matthews, may yet lead them back to the old glories—helped by the highest-priced footballer in the world: Eddie Quigley. No, North End have never been afraid to go out and get what they wanted.

After the amateurs, we have seen the hold Lancashire got on the game, but the power was becoming more evenly dispersed. Aston Villa and West Bromwich Albion struck for the Midlands; Sheffield United, Sheffield Wednesday and Huddersfield Town for Yorkshire; Newcastle United and Sunderland for the North-east, Arsenal and Tottenham Hotspur for London, and more recently, Portsmouth for the deep South.

Twice Villa have won the Cup two years in succession and, of course, six times in all. They have in fact, stamped their imprint on both the Cup and League probably more than any other club in history. They not only equalled Preston's feat of completing the double, but they have proved their greatness in old as well as modern times, though not since 1920 have they won anything outstanding.

Tales are told of the players who were sent back home to dress properly because they turned up at the ground wearing a cap or a muffler. Soccer may have passed to the masses, but its respectability was still preserved with burning zeal as much by Villa as any club. Their players had to comport themselves and play in the highest tradition.

Hunter, the Villa captain and centre-forward, had the satisfaction of scoring in their first Cup Final in 1877 against near rivals West Bromwich Albion, and from that moment there always seems to have been someone to hand over the baton to the next man. Howard Spencer took over for ten years or more and passed it on to Hampton, Bache, and Athersmith, and so on to Sam Hardy, Weston, Wallace, Clem Stephenson, Andy Ducat, Billy Walker, and latterly, Alex Massie and George Cummings.

The reputation of West Bromwich Albion has been built up mainly on English players with a few Welshmen thrown in. Until fairly recent years they never believed in Scottish importations. After Albion had beaten Preston in the Semi-Final in 1897, the outspoken Major Marindin, who refereed the match, went straight to their dressing-room and asked: " Are you all Englishmen?"

Upon being assured that they were, he then said: " Then I have much pleasure in presenting you with the ball. You have played a very good game and I hope you will win the Cup."

Little Billy Bassett—no more than 5ft. 5½ins.—preserved all those things he knew and cherished as a player when he became chairman of Albion. He and the deeply-revered Fred Everiss guided the club to that great achievement in 1931 when they won the Cup and promotion from the Second Division—the only club in the history of the game to accomplish the feat in the same season. How those two men loved their club, and how the football world loved them. . . .

Sound that rattle, ring that bell! Choose your colours, whether they be blue, red, white black, or even heliotrope . . . on to Sheffield, to United and Wednesday, whose sporting rivalry is as finely tempered as the best Sheffield steel.

United have the better Cup record—only one behind Villa and Blackburn Rovers—but Wednesday's feats in the League are more impressive. Red and white or blue and white. Wednesday have regained First Division status over United; the previous time United earned it from Wednesday also in the last match of the season. Keen? There is nothing keener between any clubs anywhere. So it should be. Sheffield has always been noted for its fighting qualities. There, they played a great part in establishing the game. They are history-makers.

While we are in Yorkshire, as it were, let us look in on Huddersfield Town, who nearly packed up before they won the Cup for the first time in their lives and followed it up by winning the League Championship three times in succession, so achieving a new footballing feat. Although they won promotion from the Second Division, they have never been relegated. It has been a fight all the way. The Huddersfield populace is divided between soccer and rugger, and Town have never fully commanded the great support which they have really earned. Huddersfield Town and Blackburn Rovers can look across the Pennines at each other in mutual admiration, keep the flag flying, and hope that one day they may enjoy those tremendous gates which others are lucky enough to have.

Once more in the football "special," we find ourselves crowded in with those joyous hearts from Newcastle and Sunderland. Now, the atmosphere takes on a sharper note. There is something lively and tingling. The speech of these enthusiasts may be less understandable than the type of football which their favourites play, but there is no mistaking its authority. They know football inside out. It's not a game with them. It's a phobia. Why, they even sit on nearby rooftops in all manner of weather if they are unable to gain admission to packed St. James' Park, and at Roker they would do the same if they could. No wonder they are crazy about the game. Over the years, they have had some of the finest talent flowing through the North-east. There is no other sport which can offer serious opposition to Soccer on the Tyne and Wear. Sunderland have enjoyed nothing else than First Division football, and although Newcastle have been in the Second Division their gates have scarcely varied. Cup and League honours have gone in full measure to both of them.

So we turn South, to Arsenal, with their modern tradition, their three League championships in succession and their three Cup victories in five appearances at Wembley. Herbert Chapman set a new style, and there is a bronze bust in the main entrance at Highbury to commemorate the memory of a great man. The name of Arsenal rings round the world. Continentals copied their colours, and others their style and methods. Beloved of their own supporters, reviled elsewhere, they have nevertheless established something which will live for ever. "The team they love to hate," is one term which has been plastered on Arsenal, and yet there is probably no club in recent times who have drawn more crowds on their travels away from home.

It is rare that a player asks for a transfer from Arsenal—why, even Bryn Jones was content to go around as twelfth man before he finally moved to Norwich. Pride of club is rightly prized by Arsenal players, past and present. Ask Alex James. Ask Joe Mercer.

The same thing stirs deeply with those Portsmouth lads who won for the club their First League championships in their Jubilee season and repeated it the following year. And those who, in winning the Cup from Wolverhampton Wanderers in 1939, defied the odds against them. Those royal blue shirts of Portsmouth can be taken as a symbol that history is made to-day and revered to-morrow.

This quick round-up of clubs unfortunately cannot embrace all. Everton, Liverpool, Manchester City, Wolverhampton Wanderers, Chelsea, Blackpool, Derby County—in fact, each and every club is loved in some way or another. The game has changed, and will continue to change, but the melody will always remain. . . .

THE ROAR OF THE CROWD

The note varies—
but it's always the Hampden spirit.

ASSOCIATION football has a common language, besides which Esperanto is an unfathomable mystery. Off-side is off-side in any land, and to the man on the terraces comparisons are made easy. The game is played to a standard pattern and to a standard set of rules so that the fan is able to look with a just eye on Jimmy Hogan's Austrian team, any Scottish team invading Wembley, and even the Dynamos. The same kind of brilliant play, the same thrills in the goalmouth, excite the men and women who pay at the turnstiles, exalting and depressing according to how their fancies lie.

Certain clubs, as has been noted, maintain their styles and traditions through the football ages, but these styles are only variations on the main theme. And the roar of the crowd—that varies too, but there is a common purpose behind it because all crowds are cheering the same thing, without being aware of it. The truth is that all the world loves a trier, and we should all be grateful that professional sport is made up of a lot of good triers.

The style of play varies, the note of the crowd changes from ground to ground: go to that compact little ground at Bury, for instance, Gigg-lane just off the main road between Bury and Manchester. You can recognise the Bury style because, although the players do not neglect good football, they have a bustling way of playing. And the crowd have their own way too—nowhere else on earth does the crowd breath that long-drawn " EE-ee " when the shot goes too wide or too high.

Go to a very different ground, lordly Villa Park, where they reckon to recognise all that is best in soccer and where they stage representative matches and Cup semi-finals, and the crowd look on with a detached air. They are aristocrats, those Villa Park fans, so much that they ought to have snub noses, turned up by Nature to scorn anything but the best. How they have loved those tussles between Matthews and Cummings, a special sort of rivalry which was always fresh, yet a link with the past and gave Villa fans their chance to sentimentalise over the great days of the nineties. Archie McLaren, most Roman of all cricketers, once sneered of a batsman whose bat was not straight: "He plays cricket like a professional footballer." One must assume that McLaren never went to Villa Park.

Travel North-east until you reach Newcastle, where they are as impartial as the Birmingham folk and where they claim they have seen the best and some-times grumble as though they are cursed with the worst! They learned to be stoical at St. James's Park before the first World War, when they failed in their great ambition to see the Cup won at Crystal Palace. Even to-day a team holding its own in the select company of the First Division is regarded as com-monplace. For the great moment they have a peculiar shout, those Geordies, which sounds like "Ha-way, ha-way", and wherever the black and white stripes of Newcastle play, you will always find a group of men who speak a strange tongue and who deliver this shout as faithfully and as fiendishly as a Maori war-cry.

Since we are using a magic carpet to cover the country, we may as well go to Portsmouth, and there for big moments they have the chant of the Pompey Chimes. And we journey just as easily and just as quickly to Wembley on Cup Final day, when among all the cries and counter-cries and some rather untidy singing there suddenly merges, calmly and strongly, the strains of "Abide With Me", one of the unforgettable moments in anyone's football experiences.

But if Wembley is an experience not to be missed, what of Scotland's Hampden Park, which has held 150,000 people whose second-half excitement has given a tag to the game: the Hampden Roar?

The Hampden Spirit! How many of the teeming thousands who pack that vast stadium on its big days recall the original Hampden: John Hampden, the man who defied authority because he thought he knew—nay, because he did know—what was the difference between right and wrong and whose independence of spirit could not tolerate confusion between the two? It is well that the name of Britain's greatest plain man should be given to the ground which holds Britain's biggest crowd, for here on a Saturday afternoon when Scotland play England every man is equal: the civic dignitaries, the distinguished Services chiefs, the officials of the various football associations, the lucky owners of tickets for the best seats—not one of them is more important than any man or woman or child standing on the highest terrace out in the rain or under the spring sunshine. Every man's opinion is as good as his neighbour's, every man's shout as loud as the next, and if the Hampden Roar, that mighty volume of sound which comes in the second half, is no longer able to send cold shivers down the spine of every English player, it is still a feature of the big games there and still wonderfully impressive.

There is a common bond between the Lancastrian who regards London as a Thames-side village and who never fails to remind anyone who will listen that football was cradled in the North; the superior Birmingham man with his mind still joined to 1897; the blue-ribboned Portsmouth supporter who bawls out his adaptation of the Pompey Chimes; the north-easterner who still speaks with awe of the all-round ability of Colin Veitch; and the wrinkled Scot who climbs to the top of the bowl known as Hampden Park. The common bond is their admiration of the one virtue every great footballer must own: courage.

It requires a big heart to put a games-player in the front rank of professionalism, and to maintain him there, and the crowd are quick to recognise this quality, quicker to spot any deficiency.

From ground to ground partisanship is built up over the years, and this type of partisanship is a good thing. There is always the longing for a home win, but the people who most hope to be able to cheer the home side off the field for a battle well won will forgive defeat if it comes about through any cause but lack of effort, lack of what they call guts.

EVERTON 6, SUNDERLAND 4

Players made the goals,
referee made the spectacle.

NO ONE can say that this or that game of football
was the finest game ever to be played, for the simple
reasons that no one person has seen them all, but on
January 31, 1935, there poured out of the gates of
Goodison Park 59,213 people who believed they had
just seen the best match of all and were firmly con-
vinced that they would never see another like it. It
is difficult to believe that any other first-class game
has combined good football, dramatic incident, and
free goal-scoring in such abundance, and those who
saw the game are never tired of re-telling the tale of
those ten goals. . . .

The draw for the fourth round that year sent Everton to Sunderland, and the teams drew 1-1, the goals
being scored by Carter and Cunliffe. That was all
the news we heard on Saturday evening but over the
week-end news filtered in from various sources that
the game had not been a satisfactory one. It had
been played with a bitterness that rather overstepped
the bounds of keen Cup-tie rivalry.

The replay was on the following Wednesday at
Goodison Park, and the game was given a treble interest. It was a Cup-tie, it was a replay of Saturday's
rather fierce match, and it was also a repeat meeting
of two teams which had met in the League at the
turn of the year a few weeks earlier when Everton
had won 6-2, against possibly the finest team of the
day.

A dozen internationals were on the field in the un-
changed teams, all imponderables since football form
varies, but one man on the pitch knew only one way:
referee Ernest Pinckston, specially appointed by the
Football Association to take charge of the replay.

One of the great referees of the day, Pinckston was fearless. It was his strength as well as his misfortune that he feared no player nor legislator either. And because Pinckston said what he thought, and said it in a forthright fashion, he was never given the Cup Final he deserved. He made possible, more than any of the players, this great fixture at Goodison. And the Football Association's reward was to deny him the one honour for which he looked forward and which he had the right to expect.

Early in the game there were signs of the previous game's bitterness—nothing rough, but pushing, jersey-tugging, an inclination to hold the ball when it was the other side's throw-in, and so on. But within ten minutes both sides were playing football . . . and three names were in the referee's note-book. By his early pounce on the offenders, he let them know that he intended to retain control; there was a clear indication that any player looking for trouble would find it . . . and receive marching orders too. The players took the hint. They settled down to play real football and if the tackling was sometimes a little less severe than the teams intended before the game, and little less deadly than their closest supporters could wish, that all helped towards the fun in the long run.

Everton won the game in the end, but they had to win it four times. They were a goal up in fourteen minutes through Coulter, a very good winger, an Irishman whose form was variable but which at its best was good enough for anyone. When Everton's left winger scored again in the thirtieth minute, the game seemed as good as won.

But just before half-time, that dashing winger Davis, equally effective even if he seemed to have few tricks compared with such men as Connor, Gurney and Carter, ranged alongside him in that Sunderland forward line, reduced the lead. Everton were nicely fixed still, but a goal just before the players go into the dressing-room at half-time is always an emphatic one, and there were doubtless serious words for both teams in that ten-minute breathing space.

Off they went again, and the football touched heights of almost unbelievable brilliance. A quarter of an hour went by while the crowd enjoyed a demonstration of all the arts and crafts of forward play from both sides and then the tiny Alec Stevenson, a Mickey Mouse sort of player, made it 3-1. Surely Everton now had the game won? For the second time their supporters felt reasonably safe, but four minutes later Connor pulled back a goal for Sunderland.

Jimmy Connor was a one-footed player, but a few managed so well with two feet. He trundled the ball along with a particularly individual trick of movement, and many a full-back, who knew of Connor's weakness with his right foot, must have scratched his head and wondered why he had had such a poor afternoon against the Scottish winger.

So with eleven minutes to go the score was 3-2 and the football still of the highest quality. Sunderland sustained their attacks well, moving the ball along the forward line smoothly, Gallagher feeding Connor accurately, and the wing-halves Thompson and Hastings joining in to make up a seven-man attack. By comparison Everton's attacks were perhaps less well maintained, and not so frequent, with Dean spreading the ball to the wings and keeping the defence occupied in watching him as the centres came over. Perhaps there were not quite so many high centres as the international would have wished, for Geldard and Coulter both showed a fondness for the cut-in, and Dean's job this day was more to marshal the attack than to score goals himself.

Sunderland saved the game again with almost the last kick of the 90 minutes. There was loose play near the penalty area, the ball bobbed about and Everton could not get it away. Gurney, who had roamed to the wings a good deal in an attempt to disorganise the home defence, was at this critical moment in his correct position but facing the wrong way as the ball came to him. With the gambler's last throw Gurney tried a full overhead kick, and his shot was true. Sagar was completely beaten by the surprise of it, and the ball went into the net to make the score 3-3 and to compel the sides to play extra time.

Everton had already won the game twice, now they had to begin all over again. For a minute or two the players stood in groups on the touchline, the trainers lending a hand with a bootlace or wiping a muddy face with a sponge. One Sunderland official ventured to put his feet over the touchline, but Pinckston was having none of that, and with an imperîous gesture waved him away.

So they set off again on the extra half-hour, and within ninety seconds the Everton supporters, half-dazed by the turn of events, had something to shout about as, for the third time, the match was apparently put safe in the keeping of the home team, Coulter scoring to make it 4-3.

By tradition one goal in extra time should win a Cup-tie, but this was the Cup-tie different. Sunderland did not falter nor change their tactics. All five forwards were upfield, Davis dashing in, Carter prodding away, Gurney wherever the ball was or likely to be, Gallacher concentrating on feeding Connor, and Connor himself disdaining to do anything but play magical football as far removed from typical Cup-tie hurly-burly stuff as Hutton's batsmanship is from the slogging of the village blacksmith.

It was Connor who levelled things again. A sudden raid, a cross from the right, and Connor, closing in, smacked the ball first-time and truly into the Everton net. Four-four, 22 minutes to go and at this stage

Sunderland were favourites. They still sustained their attacks better than Everton, and in face of all the work they had done in chasing those will o' the wisp forwards the home wing half-backs were at last wilting. Britton, not one of the most robust of men, but a football stylist, and Jock Thomson, looked as though the flesh had had enough, though their spirit was unflagging.

Now emerged the heroes of the match. If Gurney was the hero of the first part, Charles Gee was Everton's man in extra time. It was he whose energy and skill reinforced the failing half-back line, and who stood fast in those last desperate minutes. The Sunderland attack at last broke against the barrier of Gee, and soon after the second portion of extra time had begun, Everton went ahead once more, this time not to be overtaken. Geldard was the scorer, and as he closed in it looked as though he had delayed his shot too long. But he was determined to make sure; at last his run carried him into the place he wanted, and he fired home the ninth goal of the game.

It was the end of Sunderland. Gee, the running about they had done, and the scoring feats of Coulter and Geldard were too much for them. In the very last minute Geldard got one more, a high shot which Thorpe could not cover as Dean closed in to threaten one of his headers. Dean was not wanted; the ball beat them both and it was 6-4.

So in a game of ten goals, the champion goal-scorer Dean did not bag one. Eight of them went to wingers, and the last two to Albert Geldard, a winger of speed and superb balance who was, nevertheless, too inconsistent to rank among the truly great ones of soccer. But he can, to his dying day, make two claims: he scored the last two goals in Everton's celebrated 6-4 win over Sunderland, and he put Stanley Matthews out of the English International team.

MEMORABLE CUP FINALS

From Kennington Oval
to Wembley Stadium.

WHEN Manchester United, twice behind, beat Blackpool in the Cup Final of 1948, by four goals to two, consensus of opinion was that it was the best Final ever staged at Wembley. Certain it is that judged purely on the Wembley standards, Blackpool that day would have beaten four out of five teams. It was their misfortune that they had to meet a Manchester United team which was at its peak. A Cup Final has never been conducive to the best type of football. The occasion affects the nerves of most players. Therefore, with United behind at the interval the words of their captain, Johnny Carey, that day are worthy of being immortalised — " Keep on playing football ".

United **did** keep on playing football, as they had done throughout the competition—even from that Third Round tie when they found themselves a goal down after only $13\frac{1}{2}$ seconds against Aston Villa. And no one played football better than Carey himself, one of the finest all-rounders and one of the greatest-hearted sportsmen anyone could wish to meet.

If that was the best Final ever played at Wembley, which was the best in the whole history of the Cup? Only those who saw both—if anyone did—could properly answer that question, but Aston Villa's 3-2 victory over Everton at Crystal Palace in 1896-97, the season when Villa became only the second team to achieve the " double ", has been trumpeted down the ages. All the five goals were scored in the first 35 minutes, neither goalkeeper stopped more than two shots in this period, and yet they could not be blamed for those which beat them!

That rapid scoring naturally had everyone, crowd and players alike, tingling with excitement, and when he presented the trophy after the match, Lord Rosebery said: " The scene of that match will live long in my memory."

Before an attendance of 65,024—a record for the Final up to that time—Villa had the advantage of the wind in the first half. Their centre-forward, Campbell, scored the first from an oblique angle after getting the ball from outside right Athersmith.

Everton were moved to greater effort. They slammed into their rivals until they forced an equaliser through inside right Bell, following some approach play by outside left Milward and inside left Chadwick—clever combination by all three forwards. Bell and Whitehouse were both injured when the Villa goalkeeper tried to intercept. Then Everton drew ahead mainly by a free-kick taken by right half Boyle, who placed the ball into the goalmouth, where it was diverted, presumably by a Villa defender, into his own goal.

The excitement mounted and soon Villa were level also from a free-kick. Left half Crabtree, like Boyle before him, planted the ball well in, and centre-forward Wheldon whipped it into goal—2-2!

Even if Villa were not quite at their best—a fact which may have been due in no small measure to Everton's own ability—their forwards at least were thoroughly wound up and in another terrific seige, they forced the goal which eventually won the match. Menham, the Everton goalkeeper, made a faulty clearance, with the result that Wheldon eventually got his head to the ball to force it home for a great goal.

The remainder of the first half was fought out in equally determined manner, and in the first five minutes of the second, Everton threw in everything but the goalposts to snatch an equaliser. However, Villa were prepared for it, and their full-backs, Spencer and

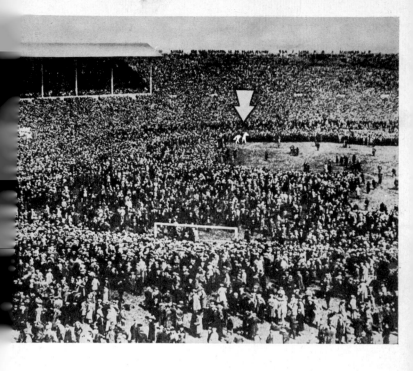

Wembley, 1923—and the cause of the all-ticket match. At the first Cup Final at the Empire Stadium the crowd broke in and invaded the pitch. British commonsense saved the day— plus the policeman on the white horse.

Photo: Sport and General.

Getting ready for the World Cup matches : the president of the Italian Football Federation, watched by F.I.F.A. officials, twirls the cage containing the numbered spheres to make the draw for the concluding stages at Rio de Janeiro.

Photo: Associated Press.

Evans, were particularly cool and magnificent. Everton took a "breather" and now it was Villa, but twenty minutes from the end Everton came back again, but try as they would, could not save the game.

Perhaps they did not reveal a full concentration of their powers in attack, and though they fought as magnificently as any side could and apparently better than most, they were not quite good enough against a team like the double champions of that year. How like Blackpool!

There was one man in that match who towered above everyone—Villa's centre half, James Cowan. That day, he played one of the best games ever seen by a man of his type. He was supported by two great backs in Spencer and Evans, and Campbell, Devey (inside left and captain), and Athersmith were great in attack.

So that was the Final which is supposed to be the best of them all. The atmosphere which affects some men so that they cannot tie their bootlaces has probably spoiled more Finals than anything else—but not all of them, fortunately.

Now, let the camera be switched to 1888-1889, the first season of the Football League, when Preston North End, thanks mainly to Mr. Sudell and the bonny Scotsmen he brought into the side, became the first club ever to complete the "double" and so set an example for Aston Villa eight years later.

In the Cup Final of 1899, Preston beat Wolverhampton Wanderers, whose first appearance it was at the Oval, by three goals to nil. Before the match is described, however, let us try to recapture some of the atmosphere through "The Free Critic," who, writing in the 'Athletic News,' had this personality piece about the Soccer enthusiast of the time and a couple of his fellow-writers :—

"There was a splendid attendance—some say 30,000,

but I will contend that there were 25.000. .... It takes a Final tie or an International to force the average Londoner to put on his 'stove pipe' and invest in a hansom; but on Saturday they drove up in shoals, whilst the rough, outspoken provincial 'fellahs' were en evidence everywhere. The 'Cackler' was along, minus, at my special request, the 16-years-old 'shiner' with which he adorned himself at the 'Varsity' sports the previous day; and the 'Bounder' arrived at 3-47 with a get-up like a real duke.

"There were some very rabid Wolverhampton people with screeching voices just behind us, and our 'Bounder' happened to get right under the jaws of the noisiest and screechiest of the whole crew. You should have seen the glances of withering contempt by the great man—they would have killed anybody but an excited Midlander, and the 'Bounder' was at last forced to give in and quit."

Here, it is important to mention that in those early days, referees for the Final were nearly always members of the F.A. council, who, if they were not refereeing or legislating, played themselves. There were also two umpires whose main duty it was to decide whether a goal had been scored or not, but it was not a satisfactory arrangement, because the referee did not have the control that he has to-day. It was not long afterwards that the system of linesmen was brought in—a much more satisfactory arrangement.

Referee for the Preston-Wolves Final was Major Marindin, who had captained two losing Royal Engineers teams in the Final and then missed his chance of leading a winning Cup team by withdrawing from the Final of 1875 because he was torn between loyalty for his regiment and his old school, Eton. In that year, the Royal Engineers beat Old Etonians after a replay. Later, the Major became Sir Francis Marindin.

The Major, as he was popularly called, had refereed the Cup Final the previous year when little West Bromwich Albion, mainly by the aid of Billy Bassett, had created a tremendous sensation by beating the might of Preston by two goals to one. Before the match, the Preston captain had asked Major Marindin's permission for the side to be photographed with the Cup, only to receive a curt: " Had you better not win it first?"

It seems that the Major had not disposed of the memory of that remarkable request even after Preston had beaten the Wolves in that 1899 Final—in presenting the trophy he complimented North End, but finished by saying that every credit was due to the Wanderers because the team was composed of local talent.

Ten minutes from time, Preston, with their superior short-passing Scottish style, so clearly had the match won against Wolves' forward rushes, wild shooting, and nervous goalkeeping, that the crowd began to encroach on the pitch to see the presentation, and the game was stopped, according to accounts, a minute or two from the allotted time because of it. One final note—when the Cup was first brought out to be presented, there were derisive shouts at its insignificance!

Preston seem destined to be concerned in out-of-the-ordinary Finals; in 1922 they were beaten by Huddersfield Town by the first penalty ever to decide such a match, and in 1938, against Huddersfield again, they themselves won by a penalty in the last few seconds of extra time, George Mutch hitting the crossbar before the ball bounced to the back of the net!

Even poor Finals can be memorable. There was, for instance, the biggest-ever victory for Bury, who in 1903 beat Derby County 6-0. Derby, beset by injuries, were without the famous Steve Bloomer that day. It was described by one writer like this: " Bury broke through the Derby defences as easily and gracefully as the fair equestrienne in the circus crashes through the hoops of tinted tissue paper held aloft by the ringmaster, what time the old grey ambles round the arena."

Derby played their worst game of the season; Bury might easily have scored two more after their sixth goal!

Then there was the robust duel between Aston Villa, making their fifth appearance in the Final in 1913, and Sunderland. This was a commentary on it :—

"The match did not by any means realise the anticipations of those who expected a very scientific game from the two finest teams of the season (they were first and second in the League). Ideas that this Final would revive the glories of ancient days (apparently the past was always better than the present, even in those days!) and would surpass in its standard of play the historic game between Villa and Everton in 1897, proved merely a dream. The Villa eleven were quite the superior team and fully entitled to their victory (1-0). The game was disappointing because science was discounted by tactics which are not in conformity with the spirit of sport or the rules of the game.

"In his interpretation of the rules, Mr. A. Adam (the Nottingham referee) was most exact and I cannot recall a Final in which I have seen so many free-kicks. . . . The Villa played an heroic game and manifested a confidence and self-possession which, allied to a considerable measure of ability, entitled them to the victory. I should say that had they had another goal they would only have received their deserts in a fast and too robust game.

"What free-kicks and stoppages entailed may be gathered from the fact that in the first half, four extra minutes were necessary, and in the second half eleven extra minutes—although five or six of these fled away when Sam Hardy was receiving attention (he fell on the ball, was accidentally injured, and had to go off for a time; Villa centre half, Harrop, temporarily took his place in goal)."

Those who talked of rough play then, and we who talk of it to-day might have been surprised by the earnest robustness of the game as it was legitimately played in the very early days. Tactics then were for a man to gain possession of the ball, stick to it and dribble with it at top speed until he lost it by a tremendous charge. From the soles of the player's boots, long, murderous spikes protruded, but there was always (we are told) a fine display of good feeling and a man would be completely hurled off his feet into the mud, only to get up with a smile and endeavour once again to get possession by the same sort of tactics!

All this happened in the very first Final of 1872 when Wanderers beat the Royal Engineers by the only goal scored by M. P. Betts, who for some reason played under the name of " A. H. Chequer." On that memorable afternoon at The Oval, Lieut. Cresswell, of the Royal Engineers, got his collar-bone broken, but with a gallantry worthy of a fine regiment and a great occasion, he kept on the field to the finish and did the utmost to assist his side!

At the conclusion of the game, hearty cheers were given and the two teams, covered with glory and a number of bruises, returned to town, where the evening was spent in gaiety. The Cup was presented to the Wanderers at their annual dinner the following month. And there were nearly two thousand spectators—so fashionable that local residents earned themselves coppers by helping the long-skirted ladies down from their carriages!

Merely as an effort to show how tough they were

in those days, a seven-a-side match was arranged some days before the Final under the auspices of the Harrow Chequers Club. That game had a bearing on the ultimate choice of the Wanderers team to battle in the Final. It started at ten o'clock in the morning and went on until four o'clock in the afternoon, and forty-seven goals were scored. After three hours of the most robust play, four men retired. Then at the end of another two hours, four others went off, but the remaining six stuck it out to the finish. One of those was C. W. Alcock.

In those days the players were dressed in the same manner as cricketers, the only difference being that some tucked the bottoms of their long white trousers into the tops of their socks. The formation was a goalkeeper, one back, one half-back, and eight forwards. And as the players were public school, university, or gallant soldier "types," they would have been affronted at the thought of doing anything but pay their own expenses.

So the wheel turned through Cup Final centres like The Oval, Lillie Bridge, Fallowfield, Everton, Crystal Palace, Old Trafford, and Stamford Bridge until, with ever-increasing crowds (a problem still unsolved), a new centre had to be found. It was—Wembley. After the first world war, Stamford Bridge was meant to be nothing more than a temporary centre for the Final; the modernisation of Crystal Palace was under discussion when the Empire Exhibition was mooted at Wembley, and the F.A. almost immediately became interested in a proposal to build a great stadium on the old golf course.

At the beginning of May, 1921, the F.A. Ground Committee visited the site and almost immediately completed a twenty-one years' agreement with the Exhibition authorities, and the following January, the Duke of York, now King George VI, cut the first piece of turf. Only sixteen months later the Stadium was opened and the first Cup Final played there. That memorable day was April 28, 1923, and Bolton Wanderers created history by being the first Wembley winners, beating West Ham United by two goals to nil amidst one of the most sensational crowd scenes of all time.

The Stadium was capable of holding 127,000 people, and that was considered to be quite sufficient. No one was properly prepared for the human flood which followed. It was not an all-ticket Final, but the events of that day compelled the stringent arrangement we now know. Getting into Wembley is easy —if you have the right ticket; otherwise, you might as well try to storm a fortress.

On that sunny afternoon—and Wembley Cup Finals have been blessed by beautiful weather—the gates were closed at 1.45 p.m. All the standing room accommodation had been filled, but there was still a multitude outside who had quite different ideas about staying where they were. They made a mass attack upon the citadel, and at 2 p.m.—an hour before the appointed kick-off—Scotland Yard was asked for a large force of mounted police and every police station in the immediate district was called upon for reinforcements.

Still this human tide poured in, clambering over walls, gates, and practically anything within their path. They invaded the reserved enclosures, the gangways, and finally the pitch. It was reckoned that there were between 200,000 and 250,000 inside the stadium that day.

It could have been the greatest disaster in sporting history, but it stands to the great credit of the good humour of the crowd, the officials, the police, and the players that nothing worse than a few minor injuries were suffered. Probably the most impressive thing of the whole afternoon was the manner in which, with confusion at its height, the crowd suddenly stood to

attention and sang the National Anthem upon the
arrival of King George V at 2.45.

The match started forty minutes late. Inch by inch,
the playing pitch was cleared. Even the players
came out to help, but the policeman on the white
horse—The White Horse Final as it has since been
called—was the most conspicuous figure in that ocean
of humanity. Slowly the lush green of the pitch reappeared, but all along the sidelines was a human wall,
into which West Ham's Jack Tresadern had temporarily disappeared just as David Jack opened the scoring after only two minutes, and which broke on the
field again slightly a quarter of an hour after the start.

The game had to be stopped while the crowd was
quickly restored to its place on the touchline again,
and at half-time the players never left the field.
Eight minutes in the second half had gone when Bolton centre-forward J. R. Smith (not to be confused
with Joe Smith, the inside left, captain, and present
Blackpool manager), collected a beautiful pass from
Ted Vizard and banged in a shot which completely
beat goalkeeper Ted Hufton, struck the spectators
crammed behind the goal-net, and bounced back on
the field.

The scenes at that fantastic match resulted in questions in the House of Commons, a committee to ex
amine the position from every angle was appointed by
the Home Secretary, and the F.A. issued the following statement:—

Association and the British Empire Exhibition, the
arrangement of the sale of tickets for admission to
the stadium (35,527), the provision of the police, and
the control of the crowd generally were in the hands
of The British Empire Stadium.

"The Football Association deeply regret the incidents and inconvenience caused to the public and will,
upon production of any ticket with any counterfoil
attached, return the cash to the holders who travelled

to the stadium and were prevented from taking their seats."

The F.A. refunded £2,797, but Wembley as a Cup Final centre had been established.

That original twenty-one years' lease has expired, of course, and a new one taken out. The first match had been the most sensational ever staged at the now-famous stadium, but turning to another aspect, what are the most remarkable goals ever scored there in Cup Finals?

There are ready replies to that question—Blackburn Rovers' goal-within-a-minute against Huddersfield Town in 1928, and the so-called centre-from-behind-the goal line which gave Newcastle United an equaliser and possibly victory over Arsenal in 1932.

In 1928, Huddersfield had had three tremendous Semi-Final battles with Sheffield United before they reached Wembley, but with an International forward line like Alec Jackson, Kelly, Brown, Clem Stephenson, and Smith, they were clear favourites to win the Cup. Blackburn also boasted such Internationals as Hutton, Jones, Healless, Campbell, Puddefoot, and Rigby, but whereas they were struggling to avoid relegation, their rivals were chasing the "double."

Rovers' real chance lay in striking quickly—and they did: rather too quickly for the liking of Mercer, Town's goalkeeper. Blackburn swept down after only a few moments of early skirmishing and Roscamp, the centre-forward, lobbed the ball forward. As it curled slowly just about the height of the crossbar, Mercer went up to catch it. Being wise after the event, of course, he ought to have punched it away, because with both feet off the ground he was suddenly knocked into the back of the net with the ball by Roscamp, who eagerly followed up.

Huddersfield were never allowed to recover from that sensational set-back. That Rovers defence would not let Town's talented attack settle on the ball, and

22 minutes after their first goal, Blackburn scored again through McLean. That Gay Lothario, Alec Jackson, was moved into the centre by Huddersfield in the second half, scored with a shot which turned over the line off an upright, but Roscamp came again to seal the issue.

By that victory, Blackburn equalled the feat of Aston Villa in winning the Cup six times. There was something else from the Town point of view—it was the first time for eighteen years that a losing side in a Final had scored.

Probably **the** most sensational goal ever scored at the Empire Stadium was Newcastle's equaliser in 1932. Arsenal were in their pomp. Only Alex James, who was injured, was missing from a star-studded team: Moss; Parker, Hapgood; Jones (C), Roberts, Male; Mulme, Jack, Lambert, Bastin, and John. Because of James' injury Bastin moved inside, a position to which he was fully accustomed. Once more, however, the favourites were to fall, but under what circumstances!

Newcastle had proved themselves great fighters, it is true, and they had some good players, including Sam Weaver, who popularised the long throw-in, yet Arsenal being what they were, only United's own supporters gave them a chance. Events, therefore, seemed to be moving towards a natural conclusion when that reliable all-rounder, John, gave the Highbury side the lead after a quarter of an hour.

How often are we reminded, especially in sport, that it is impossible to take anything for granted. United suddenly sprang into life and metaphorically exchanged blow for blow with Arsenal until all at once, the favourites were on their knees from a jolt the legitimacy of which is debated even to-day. Referee W. P. Harper considered it a fair punch, and that was the most important thing that mattered.

Newcastle centre half-back Davidson sent a long

pass down the right after intercepting a clearance by Hapgood. The ball had every appearance of bouncing over the bye-line, but Richardson, who had temporarily switched positions with his right wing partner, Boyd, galloped after it at full pace. The Arsenal defence tautened and then relaxed as the ball appeared to cross the line. In that very moment, however, they probably thought the whole Stadium had collapsed on them. Without a pause in his thrilling dash, Richardson swept the ball into the goalmouth, where centre-forward Allen, completely unguarded, headed home the equaliser. Yes, it was an equaliser. The referee was quite adamant about that. Arsenal players, too flabbergasted to move at first, began to protest until Tom Parker quickly waved his men to their places to get on with the game again—a sportsman's move and a captain's move. The rest of the game was fought at a clean, thrilling pace, with Newcastle gradually wearing down their opponents until Allen scored the winning goal.

It was not until the photographs of that bye-line incident were developed that Richardson appeared to be centring from over the line, but it was claimed that the camera had caught the incident at the wrong angle and that the ball was in the air and not on the ground as the photographs appeared to show when Richardson made his centre. In any event, the referee's decision was final.

West Bromwich Albion have had two memorable Finals at Wembley—in 1931, when they beat Birmingham and thus became the only club in the history of the game to win the Cup and promotion from the Second Division in the same season, and 1935, when they were level 2-2 with Sheffield Wednesday with only five minutes to go and were finally beaten 4-2 because of thrilling late goals by Ellis Rimmer.

Memorable Finals? Every Final is memorable. That is why the Cup is what it is—the greatest knock-out tournament in the World. Long live the Cup!

ON TOUR WITH THE F.A.

Boots instead of brief-cases—
but diplomats still.

IT IS an old jibe against footballers that they so often fail to reproduce their best form for the big occasion. The Cup Final at Wembley and the international match at Hampden Park have frequently proved disappointing if judged, not on exciting incidents, but on the general standard of combined play. But—at any rate during the past few years—to go abroad with an English team is to see football and the footballer at their best.

The professional footballer long ago stepped out of his cap and muffler. But only more recently did the pro. appreciate playing for England. For many it was a duty dance, the result did not matter, and they never cared if they were chosen again.

There was one fine player who had a consuming ambition to be selected. In due course he won the place in the international team to which his form entitled him. He played fairly well. On the way home he stated quite firmly that he never wished to turn out in the famous white shirt again, so disgusted was he with his own reception—or lack of reception! —by officials, and so disappointed was he at the spirit in the dressing room.

Well, all that has been changed. Selectors are in closer touch with the players, and have acquired the happy knack of mixing with them in hotels and addressing them by their first names. Sir Stanley Rous, secretary of the Football Association, has helped to adjust things. And the appointment of a team manager in Walter Winterbottom has welded England's chosen players into a happy family.

For the reader who can see between the lines, there is information to be gleaned in the names of the players chosen to represent England in matches abroad. The F.A. choose well-behaved players. And right away you may ask the question: what has behaviour got to do with kicking a leather ball from one end of the field to the other?

A deuce of a lot, is the answer. Firstly, the well-behaved chaps are the men who can be trusted worthily to represent England on the Continent, where every action is studied and made the matter for comment. Secondly, the intelligent fellow who can carry himself well in any company is also the man who will be receptive to coaching ideas, to team-tactical talks, is the man who will drop easily in the style of play of those around him. Brains count in football as in any other walk of life.

A grand young player was given a chance to fit in, just after the war. He did well without being a riot, and after the preliminary canters—a trip with the team as reserve, a game in a minor representative match, and so on—was put into cold storage. The need arose for a player in his position, and he was given a Continental tour. Twice he appeared in public not drunk, but a little flushed. He will not get anywhere near an English team again.

The present batch of international players—the true internationals, the dozen men who stand out—appreciate playing for England. They go to bed without being told when, they dress well but soberly, they train faithfully. It is no breach of confidence to tell this story. On the Continental tour of May 1950, England had a new rainer in Billy Ridding of Bolton Wanderers. After two days he publicly stated with warm sincerity: "These fellows don't need a trainer. They look after themselves".

On the same tour a trip from Brussels to the field

of Waterloo was planned. The match against Belgium was due twenty-four hours later. The players, of their own volition, decided to take forty winks instead of tiring themselves.

Again, on the same tour, they were at Estoril in Portugal, a glittering seaside resort known as the playground of millionaires and the resting place of exiled kings! The beach, the Casino, the gorgeous flower beds, the pools with their gigantic fish, the city of Lisbon not so far away. But for most of the time the players sat around, playing games with pencil and paper, perfectly content to rest their legs knowing that they were doing it for England.

One more example from the same tour. The "B" team were playing in Milan, and we waited in the hotel at Estoril for news of the result. At last it came through, a shattering defeat: 5-0 for Italy "B" The group of newspapermen and players turned away, speechless until two of the footballers spoke together: " Well, we'll have to roll up our sleeves on Sunday and beat Portugal ", was the theme of their comment.

Two years earlier many of these same men were in Italy, to meet the Italians in that lovely ground at Turin. They trained at Stresa, and there is the word of experienced footballers, life-long teetotallers and non-smokers, accustomed to a disciplined life, that they had never previously trained so hard for a match. This was not because they were driven to it by a stern trainer, a domineering manager, or hard-faced selectors. They did it because they realised, as soon as they arrived in Italy, that the Italians were making the match into an international political event.

Whenever an English team goes abroad, the players are hailed as " the masters ". Due homage is paid to our position as leaders in the game . . . and then behind the praise and the courtesies one realises that there is a determination, which quite often oversteps the bounds of proper sporting aspirations, to beat us. In fact, to beat us up.

This spirit was evident in Italy. In all sorts of small ways we were made welcome—social hospitality, one hastens to add, could not have been bettered —but equally in all sorts of small ways we were made aware that Italy regarded the winning of the match as a matter of national pride, as something to count eventually in the council of nations when matters of peace and war were to be discussed.

So players for England must be footballers, gentlemen, and ambassadors, too. They carry a grave burden on their shoulders, calling on them to be well behaved both on and off the field.

If the right men are chosen, this is easy off the field. But how to behave well on the field? How to avoid criticism of your style of play when you want to put every bit of vigour in your tackle, every bit of punch in our dash for goal; how to behave correctly when the referee is a man who doesn't know a push from a charge, who can't or won't see the most vicious hand-off outside the Rugby Union code; how to behave correctly when a linesman who can't speak your tongue is determined to attract attention with a wagging flag to give absurd off-side decisions?

For, take it from those who have been there—on the Continent you play the opposing team, the referee, the linesmen, the crowd, and the weather. All the cards are stacked against you, and you have to do well to win.

What do they know of football who only English weather know?

When England played Italy at Turin in 1948, they took a hammering in the first half, but led 2-0 thanks to the individual brilliance of Mortensen, who scored one goal from an absurd angle and "made" another for Lawton. It had been raining earlier in the week, and the rain was followed by a heat-wave. The weather, indeed, was such that the turf in the penalty area, laid (to the horror of those of us who inspected the pitch) only three days before the game, knit nicely in those humid conditions in time for the match.

So, at half-time, when the England players tottered into the dressing-room in a state of near-collapse after all the chasing they had done in that terrible heat, several of them wondered aloud: " Can we stick it out?".

Walter Winterbottom, the team manager, simply said: " Don't be silly, the Italians are in a worse state than you are." And he was right. The home players, who should have been able to stand up to the heat with less discomfort than the Englishmen, were at that moment standing stark naked in their own dressing-room and being sprayed from soda-water syphons. The English team pulled round, went out, and played a fine second-half to win 4-0.

English players are given spending money while abroad—and it isn't enough for champagne. It enables them to buy small gifts, but little more than that. The usual fee is £20 a match. They receive gifts at the banquet which inevitably follows the game, and how many automatic pencils and ball-pointed pens some of them have acquired I wouldn't like to guess.

There is another and happier side to the picture. The English colony always turns up trumps. They filter into the hotel, pay their respects, and try to find if there is anything they can do to make the stay more pleasant. A player may meet a friend of a friend 'way back in England, and if he is stuck for local currency and wishes to buy something, a loan or a gift may be made. And as they make their adieus, the members of the English colony don't forget to add: " For God's sake win to-morrow, or we shall never hear the last of it."

Where records were broken : the Estadio Muni-
cipal of Rio de Janeiro, where the principal
matches of the final stages of the World Cup
were played. At the deciding fixture between
Brazil and Uruguay, the host country were
beaten 2-1 before a crowd of 160,000, with gate
receipts of £125,000.

Photo: Sporting Chronicle.

And now for Helsinki. This ground was built
for the Olympic Games of 1940 which were
never staged owing to the war. Finland is now
preparing to put on the XVth Olympiad in 1952.

Photo: Olympic Games Committee.

Sometimes the tour consists of two or three matches each of first-class importance. Now and again, however, an odd game is thrown in partly with the idea of giving the players a trip, partly with a missionary zeal to show the game. Such zeal, a year or two ago, took the full English international team to two tiny grounds in Switzerland, first to Bellinzona and then to Schaffhausen. At Bellinzona the game was played on a club enclosure against a supposedly local team . . . but when the side turned out, it was found that one or two stars had been imported from across the other side of the country and there was a man whose dangerous kicking is still a by-word with the fellows who suffered. . . .

The second game took England to Schaffhausen, where a party under the trees was the social event of the tour and made one wish one had nothing else to do except sip from fragile glass, nibble biscuits, and chat to these delightful people whose beautiful town was so tragically bombed in error by American planes during the war. . . .

The game here was played on a school's pitch, and the reason was surely the most strange for turning out the full English team. A new soccer ground was considered desirable by the fans of Schaffhausen, but when a poll was taken, there was a majority against the expenditure of the money. The English team was called up to show just what a wonderful game football could be at its best. And how they fulfilled their mission! Mortensen and Matthews played at their most brilliant, Frank Swift gave one of his dizziest displays of clowning . . . and all before two or three thousand people, some of whom did not bother to pay for admission but lined the stone wall of the school playing field and looked on from the road. Soon after arriving back in England, we heard that another poll had been taken with a heavy majority in favour of building a new ground . . . and hang the expense!

There was another occasion when a big party of English players toured Scandinavia with a heavy programme. A "B" team flew across to Finland and so far as the newspapermen were concerned, the reception was not just warm but glowing. We were whisked off to a party almost before we had time to register at the hotel, and the rest of the stay was on the lines of a Bacchanalian banquet. The game, played in the Olympic stadium in a state of half-repair, was fairly easy for the English team, and the whole occasion passed off sportingly. At the end of the game a jury of experts voted on the outstanding player on each side and a presentation was made. The Englishman who received the Finnish vote was Parsons of West Ham, a young man playing for the first time for England, and if their judgement was not quite accurate through our eyes, the occasion was a happy one for a bonny little footballer.

One of the features of the crowd's attitude to the game which always impresses itself on the visitor's mind is their dislike of the pass-back from centre-half or full-back to goalkeeper. This has become an essential feature of English defensive methods, reaching its peak of perfection between Franklin and Swift and maintained by their successors, and it is far from popular on the Continent. When their own players do it, there are whistles of disapproval.

Nowadays English teams make most of their journeys by air. Sometimes players, officials, and journalists travel in one Skymaster; more frequently, they go in two parties. There used to be a suspicion that players should not talk to newspapermen for fear of indiscretions by one side or the other. Now officials of the Football Association realise that footballers and reporters are grown men and usually can be trusted. The captain, on these trips, is more important than is the skipper of a League side. He may have to make a speech, he may have to receive gifts, and he may have to do either at a minute's notice in circumstances calling for all his sang-froid.

There is marked difference in the styles of British and overseas sides. On the Continent the short pass made with the side of the foot has been developed very cleverly, but both the Italians and the Swedes have gone a long way from its slavish and monotonous use which was a feature of the football of the club teams which toured here in the 'thirties.

All Continental sides are imbued with the idea of keeping the ball on the ground and because of this, show up badly against English teams at the art of heading. But here again the Italians and Swedes are our equal and men such as Parola and Gunnar Nordahl would slip very easily into the best English club sides, as much as by their style as by their ability.

It is good for a footballer to have a few games with the English international team, good for him even to travel with them as reserve. The F.A. have acted wisely in this respect; for instance, that clever young forward and extremely likeable young man Redfern Froggatt went on the Continent in May 1950, and I don't think he stood the slightest chance of playing unless one of the others had been hurt. But mixing with them showed him how they travelled and lived, it gave him a taste of Continental crowds with their shrill whistles, and prepared him for the day when he will gain the cap his ability deserves.

Players who have been through this experience return to their club sides better players than when they left. They talk football to the others, they gain fresh ideas, add variety to their play, in fact "grow up" in a football sense. He would be a dullard indeed who could not benefit from such an experience, and that goes for newspapermen too.

How Uruguay won the World Cup
for the second time.

The fourth World Cup competition, the most glittering football fiesta of all time with its fireworks, sensations, and tremendous crowds, was won by Uruguay in Brazil's beautiful Rio de Janeiro. Thus they repeated their triumph in the first-ever World cup in 1930 and so share with Italy (also twice winners) an all-Latin domination in this great Soccer tournament.

In beating the favourites, Brazil, by two goals to one in the deciding match in the final pool, they provided a bigger sensation than England's defeats by America and Spain and Italy's reverse by Sweden's part-time amateurs. It was a remarkable ending to a remarkable spectacle.

A record crowd of 160,000 people, who paid £125,000 (easily a record for any football match in the world), were there mostly to celebrate a Brazilian victory. More than 5,000 policemen, supported by special units of the Army, Navy, and Air Force, were under orders to prevent scenes like those at Brazil's previous match against Spain, when two persons died and 260 fanatical fans were injured in a rush for seats.

Most of that vast crowd on the last memorable afternoon were there to make it a Brazilian feast. It ended as a Brazilian football funeral. So certain were the Brazilian supporters that before the game they had written and recorded a victory samba entitled " Brazil the Victora." There seemed much justification for all this optimism when Brazil took the lead just after half-time. With the Uruguayans vainly appealing for offside to George Reader, the British referee, the

Brazilian fans went wild with delight. Rockets and fireworks zoomed and banged all over the stadium and Vérey lights shot into the sky!

But after 63 minutes, Uruguay equalised and then scored the winning goal in the closing stages. The Brazilian players, who had expected to earn gold medals and thousands of pounds by winning the World Cup, trooped slowly off the field with their heads bowed, while the Uruguayan fans waved their handkerchiefs in farewell—an old South American soccer custom which the English team had experienced.

The stadium announcer was so dumbfounded that he forgot to broadcast the result of the remaining match between Spain and Sweden to decide minor placings. The Brazilian crowd was so heartbroken that men and women wept in the streets and the doctors said that they had treated 169 people for fits of hysteria and other trouble. Even Brazil's centre-half had to issue a denial that he had committed suicide, so rife was Rio with rumours!

As for the Uruguayan players, first they embraced one another, then they hugged Referee Reader, who had controlled the match firmly, and then, after receiving the Cup from the donor, M. Jules Rimet, of France, danced round the ground, gesticulating with joy. It was the turn of their supporters to let off the fireworks. . . .

From the English viewpoint, the fourth World Cup was a complete failure so far as the results were concerned, but we learned many lessons. We scored only two goals in the only three matches we played—in the preliminary pool—won one match and lost two. Both those goals, in fact, came in our first game against Chile and were scored by Mortensen and Mannion. What proved to be the biggest blow to British pride was the 1-0 defeat by the United States, the 500-1 outsiders who never won another match!

The British colony who worked at the gold mines at Belo Horizonte had made special preparations to entertain the English team, even taking up a concrete cricket pitch to ensure that the players could train on a full-size ground. But for England, it was " Lost Horizon." The American team, with a British player, McIlvenny, at right half-back—he was a winger with Wrexham before going to the United States, where he attracted the attention of Matt Busby, who was on tour with Manchester United—surprised everyone by their speed and ability.

The soccer world was astounded by America's victory, which gave rise to considerable speculation about what that country of remarkable resource would achieve if they seriously took up the game. Certainly, there had never been any previous hint of their capability of beating a full England team.

So now the situation was that in their last match in the preliminary pool, England had to beat Spain to have a chance of reaching the final series. No less than victory, which would have earned a replay with Spain, was required. But such was not to be. Once more we were beaten 1-0, and England were waved out of the World Cup, like Brazil later. At once was it realised that the unchallenged soccer supremacy which hitherto was ours—like so many other sports we had introduced to the world—was no more. At the very least, we would have to wait four years before the next World Cup was played ere the chance for atonement was provided.

Messages from Madrid stated afterwards that Spain's Caudillo had not heard so many cries of " Vive Franco!" from outside Spain since he assumed power over eleven years previously. The Spanish broadcaster from Rio, the President of the Spanish Football Association, various other officials, as well as sports writers of Spain's leading newspapers, all ended their speeches before the microphone with loud cries of "Vive Spain! Vive Franco!" Is there anyone now who doubts that political pride does not enter sport? And afterwards, Brazil beat Spain 6-1!

The swift downfall of Italy was another shock. Sweden, winners of the Olympic Games soccer title and trained and coached by the former Bury winger, George Raynor, were the only team from the Northern countries to get through to the final series, in which they finished third and gave further proof of their chances of winning the Olympic title once more at the Helsinki Games in 1952.

Uruguay played only four matches all told because they had only one fixture against Bolivia in their preliminary pool, but the one great feature arising out of the fourth World Cup was that England failed to reveal that shooting ability for which her teams are noted.

Two goals—against the twenty-two which Brazil scored all told. . . . Clearly, there is a lesson in that. Have we gone too much on defence?

The England players who went to Rio, together with their appearances, were:—

Williams (Wolverhampton Wanderers) ...	3
Ditchburn (Tottenham Hotspur)	0
Ramsey (Tottenham Hotspur)	3
Aston (Manchester United)	2
Scott (Arsenal)	0
Eckersley (Blackburn Rovers)	1
Wright (Wolverhampton Wanderers) ...	3
Hughes (Liverpool)	3
Dickinson (Portsmouth)	3
Nicholson (Tottenham Hotspur) ...	0
Taylor (Fulham)	0
Watson (Sunderland)	0
Cockburn (Manchester United)	0
Milburn (Newcastle United)	1
Mortensen (Blackpool)	3
Bentley (Chelsea)	2
Mannion (Middlesbrough)	2
Finney (Preston North End)	3
Matthews (Blackpool)	1
Baily (Tottenham Hotspur)	1
Mullen (Wolverhampton Wanderers) ...	2

Here are the complete results, with tables:—

PRELIMINARY SERIES
POOL A

Brazil, 4 — Mexico, 0 .... (at Rio de Janeiro)
Yugoslavia, 3 — Switzerland, 0 .... (at Belo Horizonte)
Brazil, 2 — Switzerland, 2 .... (at Sao Paulo)
Yugoslavia, 4 — Mexico, 1 .... (at Porto Allegre)
Brazil, 2 — Yugoslavia, 0 .... (at Rio de Janeiro)
Switzerland, 2 — Mexico, 1 .... (at Porto Allegre)

POOL B

England, 2 — Chile, 0 .... (at Rio de Janeiro)
United States, 1 — England, 0 .... (at Belo Horizonte)
Spain, 1 — England, 0 .... (at Rio de Janeiro)
Spain, 3 — United States, 1 .... (at Curytiba)
Spain, 2 — Chile, 0 .... (at Rio de Janeiro)
Chile, 3 — United States, 2 .... (at Recife)

POOL C

Sweden, 3 — Italy, 2 .... (at Sao Paulo)
Sweden, 2 — Paraguay, 2 .... (at Curytiba)
Italy, 2 — Paraguay, 0 .... (at Sao Paulo)

POOL D

Uruguay, 8 — Bolivia, 0 .... (at Belo Horizonte)

POOL TABLES
POOL A

	P	W	L	D	Goals F	A	Pts
Brazil	3	2	0	1	8	2	5
Yugoslavia	3	2	1	0	7	3	4
Switzerland	3	1	1	1	4	6	3
Mexico	3	0	3	0	2	10	0

POOL B

	P	W	L	D	Goals F	A	Pts
Spain	3	3	0	0	6	1	6
England	3	1	2	0	2	2	2
U.S.A.	3	1	2	0	4	6	2
Chile	3	1	2	0	3	6	2

POOL C

	P	W	L	D	Goals F	A	Pts
Sweden	2	1	0	1	5	4	3
Italy	2	1	1	0	4	3	2
Paraguay	2	0	0	1	2	4	1

POOL D

	P	W	L	D	Goals F	A	Pts
Uruguay	1	1	0	0	8	0	2
Bolivia	1	0	1	0	0	8	0

FINAL SERIES

Brazil, 7 — Sweden, 1 .... (at Rio de Janeiro)
Spain, 2 — Uruguay, 2 .... (at Sao Paulo)
Brazil, 6 — Spain, 1 .... (at Rio de Janeiro)
Uruguay, 3 — Sweden, 2 .... (at Sao Paulo)
Uruguay, 2 — Brazil, 1 .... (at Rio de Janeiro)
Sweden, 3 — Spain, 1 .... (at Sao Paulo)

FINAL TABLE

	P	W	L	D	Goals F	A	Pts
Uruguay	3	2	0	1	7	5	5
Brazil	3	2	1	0	14	4	4
Sweden	3	1	2	0	6	11	2
Spain	3	0	2	1	4	11	1

The next World Cup series are due to be played in Switzerland in 1954 and in Sweden in 1958. The competition was conceived in 1928 at Luxembourg and first staged in Uruguay two years later. Officially, it is named the Jules Rimet Cup, after the president of F.I.F.A., and although planned to be held every four years, the tournament was suspended for 12 years owing to the intervention of the last war.

It arose out of an Olympic Games dispute. The Olympic Soccer tournament was considered unofficial because of the various interpretations given to amateur status, and F.I.F.A. decided to stage their own world-wide competition without any restrictions on the classification of competitors. As Uruguay had triumphed in two consecutive Olympic contests, it was decided therefore to honour that country with the organization of the first World Cup in Montevideo in 1930. Out of the thirteen countries which took part, Uruguay won and thus completed their historic hat-trick.

By 1934, when the Finals were held in Rome, the entry had grown to 29, and Italy beat Czechoslovakia in the Final only after extra time. Four years later, the World Cup was held in France, but although there were more entries than ever (36) only 25 lined up for the preliminary round. U.S.A., Japan, Bolivia, Colombia, Porto Rico, Mexico, and San Salvador withdrew.

For the first time, the previous winners and the host nation, France, were excused the preliminary matches. Italy won again, this time from Hungary, with Brazil third.

Details of those first three World Cup competitions are :—

URUGUAY, 1930

Semi-Final

Argentina, 6; U.S.A., 1; **Uruguay,** 6; Yugoslavia, 1.

Final

Argentina, 2; **Uruguay, 4.**

Total Participants (13): France, Mexico, Argentine, Chile, Yugoslavia, Brazil, Bolivia, Rumania, Uruguay, Peru, U.S.A., Belgium, Paraguay.

ITALY, 1934

First Round

Italy, 7; U.S.A., 1; Spain, 3; Brazil, 1; Austria, 3; France, 2; Hungary, 4; Egypt, 2; Czechoslovakia, 2; Rumania, 1; Switzerland, 3; Netherlands, 2; Germany, 5; Belgium, 2; Sweden, 3; Argentina, 2.

Second Round

Italy, 1:1; Spain, 1:0; Austria, 2; Hungary, 1; Czechoslovakia, 3; Switzerland, 2; Germany, 2; Sweden, 1.

Semi-Finals

Italy, 1; Austria, 0; Czechoslovakia, 3; Germany, 1.

Final

Italy, 2; Czechoslovakia, 1 (during extra time).

Total Participants (29): Haiti, Cuba, Mexico, Brazil, Argentine, Egypt, Palestine, Sweden, Estonia, Lithuania, Spain, Portugal, Italy, Greece, Bulgaria, Hungary, Austria, Poland, Czechoslovakia, Yugoslavia, Switzerland, Rumania, Eire, Holland, Belgium, Luxembourg, Germany, France, U.S.A.

FRANCE, 1938

First Round
Switzerland, 1:4; Germany, 1:2; Hungary, 6; Dch.E.Indies, 0;
Sweden, Bye; Cuba, 3:2; Rumania, 3:1; France, 3; Belgium, 1;
Italy, 2; Norway, 1; Brazil, 6; Poland, 5; Czechoslovakia, 3;
Netherlands, 0.

Second Round
Switzerland, 0; Hungary, 2; Sweden, 8; Cuba, 0 France, 1;
Italy, 3; Brazil, 1:2; Czechoslovakia, 1:1.

Semi-Finals
Hungary, 5; Sweden, 1; Italy, 2; Brazil, 1.

Final
Hungary, 2; Italy, 4.
For 3rd and 4th places: Brazil, 4; Sweden, 2.

Total Participants (25): Germany, Sweden, Estonia, Finland,
Poland, Norway, Eire, Yugoslavia, Bulgaria, Switzerland,
Portugal, Hungary, Palestine, Greece, Czechoslovakia,
Bulgaria, Austria, Estonia, Lithuania, Belgium, Holland,
Luxembourg, Netherlands, East Indies, Brazil, Cuba.

In the 1950 World Cup series, England, Ireland,
Scotland and Wales entered for the first time out of
thirty nations. The long-standing International
Tournament was used as a zonal qualifying medium,
and although Scotland, finishing second to England,
earned a place at Rio, she refused to go. Her conditions were that she would participate in the World
Cup Finals only as British Champions or joint-cham-
pions, and despite pleas from England, Brazil, and
the Organizing Committee, she refused to be moved.

In point of fact, just one goal prevented Scotland
from flying down to Rio. The deciding match of the
International Tournament England beat Scotland by
the only goal. Most people believed that Scotland im-
posed too great a responsibility on her own players
in that match at Hampden Park.

First World Cup match ever to be staged in Britain was between Wales and England at Cardiff, when two players were rather badly injured and people first began to have doubts about linking the World Cup with the British Tournament. Fortunately, however, there were no further incidents to substantiate that view.